Consecrated Celibacy

A Fresh Look at an Ancient Calling

— CHRISTINE BARNABAS —

Sacristy Press

Contents

Preface

Why would anyone want to write a book about consecrated celibacy? Is it a relevant topic in this day and age? As you can imagine, I believe it is. As so many spiritual seekers across the world find meaning and sustenance in discovering the wisdom of spiritual practices that have been handed down to us through the ages, I sense that a fresh look at an ancient calling can unearth treasures which help us to live meaningfully in the twenty-first century. There are many reasons why I have felt compelled to write about consecrated celibacy. The one which stands out most clearly is that in the last few years, I have met an increasing number of people who feel called to give themselves to God as consecrated celibates, without sensing a vocation to enter a traditional, religious order. But they often do not know who to turn to or have not found a book that discusses their particular questions. This adds to the uncertainty about their vocation: does God give an invitation to such a life choice? Was it even a possibility? Did they hear correctly? Was it valid, *without* wanting to join a traditional religious community? Others have never heard about or met anyone from a religious order. They struggle to grasp what it is that God is inviting them to. One person expressed this stirring inside her in this way: "I feel God says that he wants to marry me, but what does that mean?"

The relief is tangible when people hear that there *are* others who have experienced a similar call from God. And for some that means what until now they only have been exploring tentatively becomes a real possibility: making a commitment to remain single, without leaving everything behind to join a religious order. Maybe, after all, what they sensed to be a vocation for their lives does exist?

It is often the lived example of others that allows us to trust our own intuitions or gives us the courage to step out in faith. In the case of my own journey, it was a friend's public commitment to consecrated celibacy which gently encouraged me to revisit my own calling again after nearly twenty years of having no clear sense of it. If you are considering such a life, allow me therefore in the following pages to share some of my story with you.

My first sense of having a vocation to lifelong celibacy arose at the tender age of seventeen, when I was living in my native Germany. At that time, I was part of a youth group in the Lutheran Church which had many links to celibate and mixed communities in Germany and Switzerland. Most of those communities, in contrast to some more traditional religious orders, are very "young" and predominantly independent in nature. In our youth group, we were encouraged to pray about a future calling to marriage or celibacy. I am aware that this is not quite the norm in most institutional churches! I clearly remember how I was inspired by people who had chosen to remain single; most of them I had met radiated the love of God. My initial sense that this life was meant for me started when the verse in Romans 12.1 "to give your bodies as a living sacrifice" spoke to me about giving myself to God completely as a consecrated celibate. I did some testing and stayed in conversation about this sense of vocation with people who knew me well. Eventually, aged eighteen, I felt that God was indeed calling me to this state of life. In a second step, I tried to identify which community I was meant to join. Eventually, I felt led to become a member of a community of religious sisters. They had, amongst other ministries in Germany and abroad, a nursing home where I worked during my gap year. In agreement with the leading sister at the time, it was decided that I would stay in touch with the sisters on a regular basis, whilst studying social work and continuing to be part of the Christian group in my home town. One of the sisters became my spiritual mentor during this time. Towards the end of my four years of study, the lead sister suddenly advised me that she felt I was not meant to join the community. This came as a complete shock to me. It threw me into the first major crisis in my relationship with God. Had I misheard him so consistently for more and America. In the United Kingdom, new monasticism has recently been given more attention, particularly in the Church of England. Here, Archbishop Justin Welby continues to drive the formation of such communities, particularly aimed at young people.

And here is the point: I have long been baffled by the fact that my own Northumbria Community, and the new monastic movement as a whole, have been completely silent about consecrated celibacy as an essential and integral aspect of *traditional* monasticism. In the hope of not sounding too simplistic, it should suffice for the purpose of this book to describe "new monasticism" as an attempt to seek out the wisdom of the "ancient paths" (Jeremiah 6:16) and apply it to our *way of living* in the twenty-first century. We can learn so much from those who have gone before us. Committing to a rule of life, as most traditional monastics do, can help us intentionally to foster a way of living that puts the search for God at its centre. Establishing a rhythm of prayer, intentional discipleship and engaging with our inner being are hallmarks for communities who see themselves as part of the "new monastic" movement.[1] Some of them share their lives in a common home or live in close proximity, and others, as in the Northumbria Community, live out a shared rule of life as a dispersed community. In summary, there is a realization that there are manifold riches to unearth from traditional monasticism which can inform and transform our lives today.

For centuries, it was unheard of to separate monasticism from consecrated celibacy. By definition, nuns and monks were men and women who had given themselves to God completely, making vows of poverty, chastity and obedience, the last of which meant that they were committed to perpetual celibacy. I doubt whether anyone would seriously question that promised, consecrated celibacy traditionally has been a defining touchstone for monastic life. To my knowledge and amazement, though, this aspect of monasticism has not fully "filtered through" when we engage with the wisdom and ways of the monastic living of old and try to interpret and apply them to the new monastic movement. We do not consciously explore whether the people and saints from whom we draw inspiration became who they were—at least in part—*because* they gave themselves to God in this way. If this was the case, should we not then want to ask how we can translate this crucial aspect of their vocation into this day and age, too? We do this readily with so many other facets of monasticism; for example, how can we lead a life where seeking God is the "only one thing" (Luke 10:42)? How can a rule of life help us to inform our choices and decisions in daily life? How can we weave a rhythm of prayer into our lives? How can we guard ourselves against the ever-increasing demands of consumerism, over-consumption of the earth's resources and a failure to live in harmony with creation?

A potential answer to the question of why consecrated celibacy is not specifically addressed, even in the new monastic movement, dawned on me whilst in the process of writing this book, when I engaged again with the writings of Dietrich Bonhoeffer, a German Protestant theologian who was killed by the Nazis in 1945. He is often quoted by communities who identify with the new monastic movement to explain their raison d'être:

> The restoration of the Church will surely come only from a new type of monasticism which has nothing in common with the old but a complete lack of compromise in a life lived in accordance with the Sermon on the Mount in the discipleship of Christ. I think that it is high time to gather the people for this.[2]

In his book *The Cost of Discipleship*, in the chapter on "Costly Grace", Bonhoeffer examines the role of traditional monasticism in the process of secularization of the Church, where receiving God's grace no longer included following Christ whatever the consequences. He states that the Roman Catholic Church attempted to keep a sense of costly grace by tolerating monasticism on its edges:

> In that way, monasticism became a tangible protest against the secularization of Christendom, against the cheapening of grace.

But because the Church only endured this process rather than letting it evolve to its fullness, it relativized it. Even more, the Church justified her own secularization from that process, for now the monastic life became the special achievement of a few individuals, to which the mass of church folk could not be obliged ... Doing this, the Church managed to deflect any criticism of her secularization by referring to the possibility of the monastic way of life within the Church. The fatal error of monasticism was not ... that it walked the graced path of a strict following of Christ. Rather, monasticism moved away from its Christian origin because it let its way of life become a freely chosen and special achievement of a selected few, which bore special merits.[3]

Bonhoeffer describes how Martin Luther's journey *through* the monastery back into the "world" laid open how the world came to regard the religious life as somehow a holier way of following Christ. In Bonhoeffer's view, Luther's mission was to put discipleship of Christ back to where it belonged: in everyday life, in the context of ordinary men and women, accessible to all. Family life was a place for discipleship, just as much as monastic communities of celibates. It is exactly this drawing of monastic principles into the everyday circumstances which lies at the heart

We need to remind ourselves, and be reminded by trusted friends, again and again, that our ultimate destiny is not happiness *à deux*, or living as a closely knit nuclear family but union with God and *all* s/he has created. That is the ultimate destiny of us all. Christ, while being with us in the human form of Jesus of Nazareth, was concerned about reconciling us with God, correcting the image we have of God through word, deed and embodiment. He teaches those who follow him what it means to live under "the reign of God". By doing so, Jesus Christ threw overboard many of our misconceptions of a "normal" life. And that includes our understanding of singleness, family and marriage!

In the following chapters, I provide a brief overview of what scripture has to say about the single life in general terms and committed celibacy more specifically. I then take a look at the history of men and women who consciously gave themselves to God as consecrated celibates. After exploring in more depth what I mean when speaking about "consecrated celibacy", I discuss the practical aspects of how a vocation to consecrated celibacy can be explored through discernment, formation and making a commitment. Although in no way being the only aspect of a discernment process, our approach to and experience with sexuality hugely impacts on our choices. In my view, it is therefore necessary to look at this in more detail whilst considering a vocation to consecrated celibacy, particularly as our real struggles and questions are easily overlooked in materials used in discernment. So far, I have not come across literature in that context that brings the "real questions" into the open, puts it into the wider context of how we live with our bodies and discusses the shame which is attached to anything relating to our sexuality. Whilst we live in an increasingly sexualized society, shame remains an unspoken reality. I am aware that the approach and questions raised in the chapter on sexuality is not conforming to traditional views, especially with regard to pleasure and masturbation. It is my deeply held conviction, though, that unless we dare to look at this topic with an open mind and in "fresh ways", we remain held in a negative image of our own bodies and the good, God-given gift of our sexual energy.

It is my hope that any single person reading this book would be encouraged. For those who might be called to consecrated celibacy, and for those who accompany someone on this journey, I want it to be a helpful resource. As I said earlier, I have in mind particularly spiritual directors, who in all likelihood might be the first to hear those tentative expressions of a directee towards a vocation of remaining single, sometimes even without understanding these themselves. Where there is no awareness of a calling to consecrated celibacy as a state of life, those quiet and gentle movements in the heart of someone who is drawn to such a commitment can easily be missed. It is my prayer that this book will help to raise awareness of a vocation to consecrated celibacy, both within the new monastic movement and the wider Body of Christ. Only then will we be able to help those who have been given this gift, to identify, name and live it out—to the glory of God, for their joy and the good and blessing of the world!

Naturally, I am writing this book as a woman, and I know that my perspective on the subject is significantly influenced by my specific experiences as a woman. I am aware that having a white, European background has shaped the lens through which I write, and that someone from a different gender, ethnicity and cultural background will in all likelihood perceive the themes raised in this book quite differently. I would like to think, though, that the book is still relevant to anyone who feels drawn to explore a calling to consecrated celibacy, no matter their background.

One word about "God language": After much internal wrestling about how to approach this in my book, I decided to speak of God in both female and male terms. I use attributes interchangeably, and sometimes both at the same time. I trust that this does not hinder the flow and reminds us that God always "is like . . . " and "is beyond".

Singleness and celibacy in the Bible

The Bible is fairly silent on the question of being single. This is because in the times and cultures in which the books of the Bible originated, "singleness" as we now know it was inconceivable and, especially for women, simply did not exist as a choice. However, if we look carefully, we can see how from its first pages the Bible affirms the single life. It all depends on which glasses we are using to look. The story of creation speaks about our need to be connected. Just after God called all of creation "very good" (Genesis 1:31), he says, "It is *not* good for the man to be alone" (Genesis 2:18, my italics). We must not belittle our need for belonging to other human beings, particularly when we consider that God uttered those words when humans were in perfect harmony with God. Longing for another is deeply wired within us, put in there by the Creator herself. The Christian affirmation of God being "Trinity" began to be more explicitly articulated in the third century, and we are still working out its meaning for us. If God "is more a verb than a noun"[7] as Richard Rohr keeps reminding us, being created in the image of God, at its core, is to be created for and in relationship. How then do we participate in this divine, trinitarian dance? This question is relevant to all of us, no matter which state in life we are in. God being relationship reflects something of "their" divine longing for us: an indication that for love to exist, there must be something in us, and subsequently also in God, that wants, seeks, desires, yearns and without which is incomplete. I leave that for you to contemplate.

The scripture that it is " . . . not good for the man to be alone" does not mean that the coming together of man and woman in a physical way is humanity's ultimate and *only* destiny. If we are created for relationship, then we are all created for belonging, being seen, heard, touched and known. So much so, that if we do not receive any of these in our first weeks and months of life, we either die or will, in all likelihood, be severely damaged for the rest of our lives.[8] Belonging and relating is lived out in a multitude of ways other than physical, sexual union. The commandment to "be fruitful and multiply", which is first given to the fish in the sea and then humanity, who are created "in the image of God . . . male and female" (Genesis 1:27), is not to be exclusively understood as a command to procreation. I believe it can be seen as part of God's *blessing* on humankind to join her in co-creation. Think of the word "procreation". The prefix "pro" means "taking care of", "in place of, on behalf of": We are invited to join God in the creative process. If we were to interpret God's commandment only in terms of having children, any woman or couple who can't or doesn't conceive would be completely missing their God-given purpose—which actually was the understanding we encounter as we move further into the Old Testament, and of which we still find resonances today in the Christian world.

God's covenantal promise and blessing was to come to the nations through Israel, and in particular through the physical offspring of Abraham. A mark and confirmation of God's covenantal blessing for every Israelite was therefore tied to offspring through marriage and subsequent inherited possession of the land. As a consequence, in Old Testament times it was unthinkable to remain single. Not to have children was perceived as an indication that the couple were breaking God's covenant in some way. Not to marry equalled a rejection of God's command and a refusal of God's blessing. Barren women bore great shame.[9] Unmarried women and widows literally had no means of economic survival without the support of relatives, which was the reason we can find many Old Testament warnings against the mistreatment of widows (see for example Exodus 22:22–4). Men who did not marry were seen as being disobedient to God.

However, even in the progression of the Old Testament we can see that God points to a different and bigger picture by introducing in the prophet Isaiah the hope of a particular, single "seed of Abraham". The Songs of the Servant indicate that there is *one* person who will carry the blessing, rather than a whole nation through whom the nations of the earth will be blessed. It is here that we hear the Song of the Barren Woman (Isaiah 54:1–5) who is promised to have more children than the woman who is married:

> 'Sing, O barren women, you who never bore a child;
> burst into song, shout for joy,
> > you who were never in labour;
> because more are the children of the desolate woman
> > than of her who has a husband', says the LORD.
> 'Enlarge the place of your tent, stretch your
> > tent curtains wide, do not hold back;
> lengthen your cords, strengthen your stakes.
> For you will spread out to the right and to the left;
> > your descendants will dispossess nations
> > and settle in their desolate cities.
> Do not be afraid; you will not be put to shame.
> Do not fear disgrace; you will not be humiliated.
> You will forget the shame of your youth
> > and remember no more the
> > reproach of your widowhood.
> For your Maker is your husband—
> > The LORD Almighty is his name—
> the Holy One of Israel is your Redeemer;
> > he is called the God of all the earth.

If you read this passage carefully, you can note it carries the indication of "spiritual fruitfulness". Two chapters later in Isaiah, it is the foreigner and the eunuch who are promised to be included in God's covenant—a total shock to Jewish ears:

> This is what the Lord says:
> 'Maintain justice
>   and do what is right,
> for my salvation is close at hand
>   and my righteousness will soon be revealed.
> Blessed is the one who does this–
>   the person who holds it fast,
> who keeps the Sabbath without desecrating it,
>   and keeps their hands from doing any evil.'
> Let no foreigner who is bound to the Lord say,
>   'The Lord will surely exclude me from his people.'
> And let no eunuch complain,
>   'I am only a dry tree.'
> For this is what the Lord says:
> 'To the eunuchs who keep my Sabbaths,
>   who choose what pleases me
>   and hold fast to my covenant –
> to them I will give within my temple and its walls
>   a memorial and a name
>   better than sons and daughters;
> I will give them an everlasting name
>   that will endure for ever.
> And foreigners who bind themselves to the Lord

> to minister to him,
> to love the name of the Lord,
>   and to be his servants,
> all who keep the Sabbath without desecrating it
>   and who hold fast to my covenant –
> these I will bring to my holy mountain
>   and give them joy in my house of prayer.
> Their burnt offerings and sacrifices
>   will be accepted on my altar;
> for my house will be called
>   a house of prayer for all nations.' (Isaiah 56:1–7)

In the New Testament, Paul, in his letter to the Galatians, follows the story line of "Abraham's promised seed". He clearly identifies that this seed is one person, Jesus Christ: "The promises were spoken to Abraham and to his seed. Scripture does not say 'and to seeds', meaning many people, but 'and to your seed', meaning one person, who is Christ." (Galatians 3:16).

In Ephesians 1:3–14, Paul says that it is through Jesus Christ that we are receiving our spiritual inheritance. It is an inheritance we receive in God's eternal kingdom, which in Christ *has come* to us and is "not yet" established in its fullness. In Christ, we all are blessed, fully, no matter whether we are married or not. In other words, the Old Testament's understanding that the blessing of God consisted in marriage, offspring and possession of land is no longer applicable. Neither marriage nor children are evidence of God's blessings in one's life as a result of keeping his commandments (although both marriage and children surely are a blessing!). Marriage and children now carry a significantly different meaning compared to Old Testament times.[10] They reflect something of God's relationship with his people just as the single person does, but in a different way.

The largest section on singleness in the Bible is 1 Corinthians 7. It is worth mentioning that Paul answers specific questions the Corinthians put to him, even though we do not know which questions these were. The Corinthians lived in a culture where sexual activity was pursued outside marriage, and this frequently continued after someone had married[11]—quite similar to our current culture in Western society. In his approach to singleness, Paul reinforces the sanctity of marriage. At the same time, he strongly advocated a single life, free of sexual engagement. In his view, this enabled the person freely to pursue the furthering of God's kingdom, without being distracted by legitimate concerns for family life, which those who live in that state of life inevitably experience. What Paul seems to say is that there is a specific gift of embracing singleness, a *charism*, available to those to whom it is given, and, in Jesus' words, to those who "can accept this" (Matthew 19:12). In Paul's view, the married person may be caught up in concerns " ... about the affairs of this world", and in trying to please their spouse. An unmarried person can be free to be solely " ... concerned about the Lord's affairs" (1 Corinthians 7:32-4).

Jesus, in being single himself, underlines the paradigm present in the New Testament. Being married and having children no longer is the "default position" or way of life that solely or primarily carries God's blessing and promise. No matter which state of life, the spiritual inheritance that God offers in Christ is accessible to all. Spiritual fruitfulness is something to which we are all invited.

We should not forget, though, how shocking it was in Jesus' time to stay single, and his approach to family was radically different from that expressed and expected in his society. I want to quote some of Jesus' statements about family life in full, as I believe it is important for us to appreciate *how* radical Jesus really was:

> While Jesus was still talking to the crowd, his mother and brothers stood outside, wanting to speak to him. Someone told him, 'Your mother and brothers are standing outside, wanting to speak to you.' He replied to him, 'Who is my mother, and who are my brothers?' Pointing to his disciples, he said, 'Here are my mother and my brothers. For whoever does the will of my Father in heaven is my brother and sister and mother.' (Matthew 12:46–50)

> Now large crowds were travelling with him; and he turned and said to them, 'Whoever comes to me and does not hate father and mother, wife

and children, brothers and sisters, yes, and even
life itself, cannot be my disciple.' (Luke 14:25–6)

I agree with Bonhoeffer, who notes that our families of
origin have a tendency to put a claim on our lives that
can easily distract and at times prevent us from pursuing
Christ's call to follow him. Jesus is not telling us literally
to "hate" our families, but to realize that Christ has
stepped between us and the immediate bonds of family
relations. With Christ's call on our lives, a new reality
has been created which needs to be at the centre of our
lives.[12]

In his dealings with single women, Christ also broke
with the conventions of his culture. The woman weeping
at Jesus' feet, wiping them with her hair and pouring
perfume on them, is one example (Luke 7:36–50).
Jesus rebukes his disciples when they did not believe a
single woman whom he had explicitly commissioned to
carry the message of his resurrection (John 20:1–18 in
conjunction with Mark 16:11 and 14). Jesus was surely
not a "family man" in the traditional sense of the word,
nor in his connections with his blood relatives! Having
said that, Jesus did not devalue family, and he stressed
the importance of honouring our parents.

There are only two occasions in which Jesus directly
spoke about being single:

When Jesus had finished saying these things,
he left Galilee and went into the region of Judea

to the other side of the Jordan. Large crowds followed him, and he healed them there. Some Pharisees came to him to test him. They asked, 'Is it lawful for a man to divorce his wife for any and every reason?' 'Haven't you read,' he replied, 'that at the beginning the Creator "made them male and female," and said, "For this reason a man will leave his father and mother and be united to his wife, and the two will become one flesh"? So they are no longer two, but one flesh. Therefore what God has joined together, let no one separate.' 'Why then,' they asked, 'did Moses command that a man give his wife a certificate of divorce and send her away?' Jesus replied, 'Moses permitted you to divorce your wives because your hearts were hard. But it was not this way from the beginning. I tell you that anyone who divorces his wife, except for sexual immorality, and marries another woman commits adultery.'

The disciples said to him, 'If this is the situation between a husband and wife, it is better not to marry.' Jesus replied, 'Not everyone can accept this word, but only those to whom it has been given. For there are eunuchs who were born that way, and there are eunuchs who have been made eunuchs by others—and there are those who choose to live like eunuchs for the sake of the kingdom of heaven. The one

> who can accept this should accept it.' (Matthew
> 19:1–12)

In Matthew 22:23–8, Jesus is asked about marriage at the resurrection. Sadducees approached him, questioning whose wife a woman would be at the resurrection as she had seven husbands, all of whom died:

> Jesus replied, 'You are in error because you do not know the Scriptures or the power of God. At the resurrection people will neither marry nor be given in marriage; they will be like the angels in heaven. But about the resurrection of the dead—have you not read what God said to you, "I am the God of Abraham, the God of Isaac, and the God of Jacob"? He is not the God of the dead but of the living.'
>
> When the crowds heard this, they were astonished at his teaching. (Matthew 22:29–33; see also Luke 20:34–36)

Jesus' statements about singleness are each made in the context of a discussion about a different subject. On both occasions, Jesus sets out being single in a completely new light, which at the time in Jewish culture was simply not thought to be possible. Jesus does not give a *command* either to marry or not to marry. But, for the first time in Jewish tradition, he introduces a free choice of remaining unmarried "for the sake of the kingdom". He also seems to say that both states of life are possibilities, *gifts*, that carry a mystery within that can only be found by those who live in them.[13] On first hearing, that may sound rather obvious, but living *inside* mystery in any context, and *experiencing* it, is anything but easy and something quite different from that imagined from the outside! Being married requires many a death to one's ideas and thoughts of what married life should look like and what or who the other person is, should be, or will become. Being single requires similar deaths to our assumptions and expectations of what life should be like. Getting married or staying single is not the answer to life's problems. In each state of life, we are simply presented with *different* sets of problems and struggles. Being in a committed relationship, being single and wanting a partner, or consciously embracing singleness, for the sake of the kingdom, for those "to whom it is given"—*all* carry blessings and challenges. No state in life will ever meet all of our longings.

It seems to me that marriage is, in Jesus' words, part of God's good intention for us as an expression of God's will and order of creation. But equally, being single can be an expression of the kingdom and reign of God (see Matthew 19:1–11, as quoted above). We need to be mindful that marriage finds its completion in resurrection, a time when " ... [people] neither marry nor be given in marriage; they will be like the angels in heaven" (Matthew 22:30). This is what the marriage vow intends to convey: " ... till death us do part". And it is exactly here, looking at the resurrection, that Jesus is recorded telling his audience that they "do not know the Scriptures or the power of God" (Matthew 22:29). Realizing how little is spoken about that in church, I sometimes wonder whether this is still the case when it comes to people's understanding about human marriage! All too often we hear about couples being reunited in heaven again *as spouses*. Whilst I appreciate that longing, I am certain that we will not relate to our spouses in the same way in heaven as here on earth. The biblical message we have just looked at is quite clear. The visions of a New Heaven and New Earth as they are portrayed in Isaiah 65 and Revelation 21 indicate the largeness to which we can look forward. The union we will experience there, with God, with everyone and everything, will no longer be focused on special and exclusive relationships between pairs, but will be radically different. Rest assured that no one will miss the old way of relating!

Making a deliberate commitment to celibacy can be a state or life-form with an eschatological dimension. This aspect has always been part of the meaning of taking such a vow. It points to the end of time and to God's future that will be different and much greater and larger than that which we can now know or anticipate.

I wonder whether it is here that the teachings of the Church need to change. I believe we need to foster a greater awareness that marriage is designed for the purpose of going beyond oneself, and even beyond having children. Would this not change how we share our lives and see our different states in life? We all are made for relationship and participation in a *community* of faith. Marriage is not the ultimate purpose in life, nor is having children. I know of many couples who struggle with comments about being childless and being given the impression that without children "something is not quite right". Equally, people who are single, whether by choice or not, are often seen as somehow lacking something or being incomplete. But they are complete as they are, just as anyone else is—in themselves. And consecrated celibacy is simply another option for those who are called to it. I believe that the new monastic movement, drawing precisely from the wisdom of men and women who made a commitment to remain single, is ideally placed to embody an understanding that neither marriage nor singleness is the ultimate goal in life. It is about our relationship to Christ, and, flowing from that, how we connect with each other and share our lives together, be it in a community which lives together locally or is dispersed. That opens up a new horizon. If we are God's kingdom in the diversity of all relationships, we begin to see something of the reality of God's kingdom, which is always both, the "already and not yet". Having some inkling as to how it might be to see each other in eternity and to join the great Communion of Saints will give us a new perspective on our lives. It can help us to be less clinging: we learn to let go of insisting that all of our needs must be met right now, in specific ways.

George MacDonald expressed his imaginings about our shared future like this: "I think we shall be able to pass into and through each other's very souls as we please, knowing each other's thought and being, along with our own, and so being *like* God."[14] This indeed sounds intriguing and something to look forward to, at least as far as I am concerned. Intimacy and union, being known and knowing deeply without the need for exclusive sex—great!

2

Consecrated celibacy: A brief history

Even a brief look at history tells us that from the earliest days of Christianity, there were people who followed Jesus deliberately and intentionally as single people. Although we might "know" *about* this, sometimes it does not (fully) register with us. Many people who played such a significant part in shaping Christian history were consecrated celibates. Of course, one could argue that this was not necessarily and always for the better! Especially as within a few hundred years of Church history, it was mainly celibate men who held positions of power in the institutionalized Church. Celibate women were under their authority and for most of the time only allowed to live their calling in a *cloistered* environment, once again being moved out of the public sphere.

Is this perhaps one reason, particularly in the non-Catholic world, why we put this aspect of the story aside as belonging purely to the past? We have already noted the example of the apostle Paul. Unfortunately, his approach to the body is often misunderstood.

Paul deliberately chose not to marry so that he could be totally free for God, " ... for the Lord's affairs" (1 Corinthians 7:32,34). John the Baptist was so consumed with his task of being " ... the voice of one calling in the wilderness, 'Make straight the way for the Lord'" (John 1:23), that it left no room for him to have a family. As I mentioned earlier, we should also not forget that, as far as we know, Jesus never married. At the time, and in traditional Jewish culture this was simply unthinkable and seen as not fulfilling God's foundational command to be fruitful.[15]

The first group of Christians we traditionally recognize as committed to celibacy " ... for the sake of the kingdom" (Matthew 19:12) were the Desert Fathers and Mothers. They fled from life in the city with all its temptations, at a time when Christianity had just been fully acknowledged and accepted by Constantine in AD 313. The fourth-century church father Antony has traditionally been seen as the founder of monasticism. However, even before him, men and women, and not only in Egypt but also in other places in the East, were already leading a recognized monastic life. They often lived near a village or town, or even within a city, and at times in the context of a family.[16] But for most, to follow the calling to monastic living meant to embrace staying single for God. The monastic life was very much seen as an *ascetic* path:

> The 'ascetical-monastic' type of spirituality
> sometimes prescribes special places such as the
> wilderness or the monastery. Characteristically,
> it also describes practices of self-denial,
> austerity, and abstention from worldly pleasures
> as the pathway to spiritual growth and moral
> perfection. The end in view is a condition of
> detachment from material existence as the
> pathway to eternal life.[17]

The forgoing of marriage by most who followed this pathway was a central element of this asceticism. So much so that it is hardly ever explicitly mentioned in the literature describing early monasticism.

There are differing views as to whether the Desert Fathers and Mothers brought in extreme forms of asceticism.[18] Many authors believe that their form of "exercise" (which is the meaning of ascetism) was rooted in the ordinary and aimed at a state of inner collection and rest. Others state that it was predominantly the leaders in the early Church, like Clement of Alexandria, Tertullian and Origen, who were heavily influenced and guided by Greek philosophy that had introduced a dualistic split of "body" and "soul". In any case, the Church quite rapidly embraced an extremely negative attitude towards the body and sexuality, and within a couple of hundred years sexual abstinence became a recommendation and later a requirement for male clergy. There are differing views as to when and why clerical celibacy was introduced and by which time it was firmly established. It appears that it was both seen as a spiritual discipline in "imitation of Christ" as the spouse of the Church, but equally a means of ensuring that the Church would not be materially responsible for the widows and children of priests. Clerical celibacy is still very much a life-question in the Catholic Church, more than 1500 years later!

But let us return to the Desert Fathers and Mothers. The lives of those early celibates were centred on seeking God in ongoing, solitary prayer, whilst carrying out simple manual labour. Living under regular, spiritual counsel was a vital part of such a calling. Sometimes the Desert Fathers and Mothers lived together in clusters, yet without communal prayer; in essence they were hermits. A different model of monasticism was introduced by Pachomius in c.AD 320, who founded communities of celibates who lived together under a shared rule, regular prayer times, shared meals and work. Those communities would sometimes evolve into whole villages—an approach which later would inspire St Augustine and St Benedict.[19]

It is suggested, though, that one of the very earliest expressions of monasticism in the Christian Church was the emergence of women committed to celibacy. At times, they—both widows and virgins—formed communities in an urban environment and undertook pastoral and spiritual tasks.[20] Interestingly, for many of these women, it seems that it wasn't a radical asceticism that drew them to this commitment, but rather their explicit understanding of it being "'marriage to Christ,' which entailed sexual abstinence as the outward expression of spousal fidelity".[21] Sandra Schneiders postulates that for men, the role of celibacy in their pursuit was instrumental, whereas for women it was essentially unitive, that is, integral to the end itself. [22] A friend of mine who made a commitment to consecrated celibacy as a widow put it like this: "It was not about doing anything for God. He wanted my companionship and time. It was just about him." I believe this is a valid and noteworthy observation and one to bear in mind when we look at discerning a call to consecrated celibacy later.

As a companion of the Northumbria Community, I have a particular interest in a spirituality which had its origins in Ireland, and which, although it was not a cultural or religious unit, tends to be called "Celtic Christianity". This spirituality has been seen as influenced more directly from the tradition of the Desert Fathers and Mothers than by the Christianity of the Roman Empire. It had a strong monastic feel to it and spread through Northumbria and beyond through St Aidan in the seventh century. There were communities of celibates as well as families, sharing their lives in prayer and service. Predominantly though, it was those who lived out their vocation as consecrated celibates who were key in spreading the Gospel of Christ, including St Aidan, St Hild, St Brigid and St Cuthbert, to name but a few. As they did not have any other primary commitment in their lives, they were enabled to be wholly available to God in prayer and service. They could readily respond to any call of service, or in "wandering for the sake of Christ". Yet close attention was also paid to the spiritual needs of the individual, finding its expression in the practice of spiritual guidance, or "soul friendship". This practice derived from the Desert Fathers and Mothers who put an emphasis on obedience to a spiritual father and mother. In contrast, obedience "to a Rule of which the superior was the spiritual interpreter and legal monitor"[23] became the norm for monastic celibates in the rest of Western Christendom. Another huge difference between the Celtic and Roman approach to monasticism, from the fifth century onwards, was that many monastic centres in Ireland and Northumbria were led by celibate women. This was unheard of in the rest of the Christian world. Some of these were "double monasteries", that is communities of women and men. As Edward C. Sellner points out: "What is clear from early biographies of Brigid, as well as the stories of Hild, is that such powerful abbesses exercised an influence on their times that has almost no parallel in later history— except perhaps for Hildegard of Bingen in the twelfth century and Teresa of Avila in the sixteenth."[24]

Monasticism continued to be part of the Christian landscape for centuries, though not without its struggles. Over time, many of these "became centres of spirituality, learning, and culture. They also amassed great wealth and became major players in the politics of medieval Europe. With wealth and power came corruption and intrigue which hindered the spiritual growth of the monasteries and prompted reform movements within Monasticism itself." One example of such reform movements within monasticism are the Cistercians in the twelfth century. The mendicant orders, such as Franciscans and the Dominicans lived out ideals of poverty and simplicity in new ways, away from buildings and in reaching out to a growing urban population.[25] In the sixteenth century, apostolic orders, like the Jesuits, with an emphasis on service and mission in the world, sprang up throughout Europe. From the earliest beginnings of organized religious life, for women, joining a religious order often was the only means of receiving an education. For families living in poverty, having fewer mouths to feed was behind their decision to send a child away to a monastery. Therefore it was common for monasteries to consist of individuals who had neither vocation nor desire for monastic spirituality. As a result, the original purpose of monastic life was often undermined and frequently turned into the abuse of position and power. This of course does not mean that there were no genuine vocations for the monastic life.

Alongside coenobitic monasticism, the eremitical calling to live as a hermit or anchoress continued to exist throughout the centuries. These men and women sought to live a solitary life, dedicated to prayer and

together an intense and personal love relationship with God that remained connected to the earthly and mundane. This connection to the humanity of Jesus made them bold in preaching and teaching. They felt that personal, meaningful prayer was for everyone, not only for the few. The movement nurtured many women mystics, who, at a time when devotional practices were on the rise, explored and experienced an intensely intimate and affective spirituality. This later became known as "love mysticism",[28] and Mechthild of Magdeburg was probably the most widely known of these women. In a time when women had no power, and religious life in monasteries and apostolic orders was under tight scrutiny and control of the exclusively male clergy, the Beguines' approach was extraordinary. It is of little surprise that eventually they came under suspicion of heresy.

From the fourteenth century onwards, reform movements in several European countries challenged issues of control and abuse of power in the Catholic Church. John Wycliffe in England (1320–82) and Jan Hus in Bohemia (burnt at the stake during the Council of Constance in 1415) wanted to abolish obligatory celibacy for priests and the practice of indulgences, and make liturgy and scriptures accessible in the language of the people. They had a strong influence on Martin Luther, who ignited the Reformation in Germany through his Ninety-five Theses in 1517. Parallel movements sprang up in Switzerland under Zwingli, and John Calvin's writings became an important influence in what was later called the Protestant Reformation, spreading throughout the continent in different shapes and forms.

This had a long-lasting impact not only on the Church generally, but on monastic life in particular, as most monasteries were subsequently dissolved and some destroyed. The dissolution of monasteries was both a political and economic act, but one that created a social "problem", as the nuns of dissolved convents had to be provided for. Martin Luther's marriage as a previous Augustine friar with Katharina von Bora, who had escaped a Cistercian convent, illustrates this situation. Most reformed churches allowed priests to marry. After many centuries in which the life of a monk or nun was seen as being "holier", the pendulum finally swung, and marriage and family life were now understood as circumstances where one's calling from God could be lived out.

Looking at the history of the Church of England, it is striking that monasticism was basically suppressed until its restoration in the mid nineteenth century. This gives us some indication as to how long it can take for "change" to occur in institutional settings!

Today, traditional religious orders experience dwindling numbers in the Western hemisphere and renewed interest in other parts of the world. Their emphases and charisms vary greatly, as can the motivation to join one. Although it is rare, there are modern-day hermits amongst us, and such a calling has seen a renaissance in recent years.[29]

The "Order of the Consecrated Virgins" (OCV), in the Catholic Church, has origins stemming back to committed widows and virgins in apostolic times which I mentioned earlier. The order was revived at the time of the Second Vatican Council, aiming at women outside a monastic or apostolic order. I am aware how off-putting this name might seem to many. It certainly did to me when I first came across it, and I therefore want to use Schneiders' helpful explanation of the terminology.

To describe the reality of consecrated celibacy,

> virginity was the term of preference in the earliest centuries of the Church. All of the great treatises on Religious Life from the patristic period are entitled, in one way or another, 'On Virginity'. From the beginning virginity was understood to consist not exclusively nor even primarily in physical intactness, that is, in the state of never having had sexual intercourse, although physical integrity was a powerfully expressive symbol of the spiritual reality of integrity and self-gift. . . . It was primarily a matter of faith and secondarily a physical fact.[30]

It appears, however that, particularly in the USA, there is disagreement about this approach. The American OCV expressed "deep shock" when Pope Francis in 2018 decided that widows can be consecrated as virgins. The Vatican document, entitled *Ecclesiae Sponsae Imago*, says that the "call to give witness to the Church's virginal, spousal and fruitful love for Christ is not reducible to the symbol of physical integrity".[31] I personally find this statement rather hopeful. It is moving away from the notion that (previously lived) genital sexuality would in any way "cloud" or undermine one's ability to fully give oneself to Christ as a consecrated celibate. Why would it? Maybe it is an indication how much shame we still connect with sex, and we will look at this in Chapter 5.

If you can join me in adopting a faith approach to virginity, I hope that you are more open to discover that the OCV simply is an "order" of women, who, vowing to stay chaste, under the authority of their local bishop, are given in a sacramental as "brides to Christ". Members of this worldwide order support themselves financially and offer their charism in service and ministry in the context of a local church.[32] In the Church of England, the "Single Consecrated Life" gathers and supports both men and women with a "vocation to live the single consecrated life as a response to a call from God to live out their Christian life under the vow of consecrated celibacy".[33]

Another modern-day example of how consecrated celibacy is lived out is the Melanesian Brotherhood in the Solomon Islands and Papua New Guinea.[34] In this Anglican order, the brothers take vows of poverty, chastity and obedience during a novitiate lasting for three years. Most of the brothers are not taking life vows and return to their villages and get married.

For those of us who find ourselves outside or on the edges of traditional, institutionalized church, be it Anglican, Lutheran, Catholic, or Episcopal, questions arise. With whom can we connect in meaningful ways to support us in our calling? How do we find ways of accountability, other than reporting to a bishop once a year? I will expand on this later in this book.

Of course, much more could be said about the history of men and women who have given themselves to a commitment to celibacy for the sake of God's kingdom, and in the context of monastic and religious life. It is hoped that this brief overview of past movements has been sufficient in serving the purposes of this book. It should demonstrate that throughout the centuries, God has called some of his followers to intentionally live out their singleness as one of the many charisms given to the Church. It should also emphasize that people have been called to live in that way both as members of *and* outside of a religious order.

A calling to consecrated celibacy outside a traditional religious order and/or institutionalized church setting brings us to the specific question: what do we actually mean when we speak about "consecrated celibacy"? And this is what I would now like to move on to.

3

What is consecrated celibacy?

I feel it is important to identify what "celibacy" means and what it does *not* mean, because I have found that even amongst Christians there is significant confusion about the terminology. The longer I have engaged with this subject, the more I wondered whether it is an issue because of the English language. It seems that in English-speaking countries, the word has evolved to have only one specific meaning, namely a person who does not engage in genital sexual activity. It is commonly and widely used in the United Kingdom with that meaning. As a result, some Anglican clergy nowadays publicly declare that two people living together and being partners, can do so in a "celibate relationship". Others suggest it would be helpful to talk about all single Christians who choose to stay sexually abstinent as "celibates".[35] As far as I am concerned, this is not what "celibacy" means and using the term for all single people who do not engage in sex, in my view, only makes it more complicated. For those living in a sexually abstinent relationship, I would rather call this to be in a *platonic* relationship. I believe that a "celibate relationship" between two human beings does not exist. I suggest that one can only be a celibate after having made a *commitment* to celibacy. The origin of the word "celibacy" indicates that it means to make a commitment to not marry for *religious reasons.*

"Celibacy" is derived from the Latin *coelibatus* or *caelibatus*, meaning "unmarried". This in turn stems from, or is at least closely linked to, the Latin word for "heaven", *coelus*. The German word for celibacy, *Zölibat*, makes that even clearer. In German-speaking countries, *Zölibat* is only ever used in a religious context, such as for monks and nuns or Roman Catholic priests. For example, German-speaking single people, whether sexually active or not, or whether Christian or not, would never call themselves living *zölibatär* (celibate), unless they consciously wished to live as a *religious* because of their Christian convictions. In all other circumstances, they would say they are *single* or *ledig* (which means "free"), irrespective of their beliefs about sex outside marriage. Just from a linguistic point of view, this highlights that making a commitment to consecrated celibacy "is not about not having sex, but genital abstinence expressive of the lived choice not to engage in any other relationship as the *primary commitment* of one's life (as) the symbol of the immediate and total self-gift in love to Christ".[36]

This choice is made *out of love for Christ* and "for the sake of the kingdom of heaven" (Matthew 19:12). A consecrated celibate *freely* chooses not to engage in any sexual activity with another person. Nor do they seek or have *any primary* relationship in their lives with another human being, be it sexual or platonic. Whilst by this I do not mean that a consecrated celibate should not have close friendships (quite the contrary), a significant, internal shift takes place after making this commitment which needs to be honoured and protected, and that inevitably impacts on all our relationships in life. We will explore this in more detail in Chapter 7.

Saying all this, I do not want for even a moment to give the impression that Christian singles who have not made such a commitment will not or cannot have a deep and intimate relationship with Christ, or could not choose to make their relationship with God the primary focus of their lives. In no way do I doubt someone's dedication and wholehearted following of God. But I also cannot deny that *vowing* to give oneself as a consecrated celibate to God and therefore deliberately and intentionally closing the door to the possibility of any future primary relationship for the rest of one's life creates a distinctive new state in life, just as much as marriage does. All consecrated celibates I know report the same, that making that vow moves them into a different place, both in their relationships and friendships to others and their relationship with God.

As I briefly described in the previous chapter, many scholars believe that it was unmarried or widowed women in the first three centuries AD who embodied most clearly what lies at the heart of consecrated celibacy. Their focus was *not* the foregoing of sexual activity or the exercise of ascetic practices. Nor was it primarily about joining a community or participating in a certain ministry. For them it was about preserving one's whole self, body, soul, and mind, to be given completely and in freedom to the person of Christ. As we explored, the term most frequently used in the early Church to describe this act of total self-giving was "virginity". The original use of the term was precisely *not* about emphasizing physical intactness or not ever having engaged in sexual activity, but rather the radical preservation of oneself *for the relationship with God*. This self-gift was not a means to an end, but an outward expression of the experienced union with Christ. And this is why, for many, only the metaphor of "marriage to Christ" and being a "bride of Christ" captures "the totality, exclusivity, and fecundity of the commitment as well as its deepest source in the love as strong as death that fuels the life-encompassing God-quest".[37] This should give us an indication that the nuptial metaphor for many women who have made such a commitment is not an expression of being made subordinate, quite the opposite. They experience being "brides of Christ" as being drawn ever more deeply into a relationship that is marked by equality and mutuality. This goes against what churches historically—and still in some denominations—have taught about the woman being subordinate to the husband as her "head". When God is experienced as an equal for the first time, it often comes as a surprise and can even cause fear, particularly in women, as we are not used to hearing "that God also desires a relationship of radical mutuality with human beings".[38] As we will see later, we need a spiritual director who can recognize a sense of developing mutuality with God. The spiritual director needs to be able to work with whichever imagery the person drawn more deeply towards God uses to describe what is ultimately beyond words, or gently name that this might be what God is inviting the directee to. To avoid any confusion, I am not talking about us being the same as God, but a sense of God wanting to live and work with us in a *partnership*, and in that sense treating us as equals.

Over time, as religious life became more institutionalized, it seems that many people who entered it sought to become part of a specific community, and perhaps to give themselves to a particular ministry. As already mentioned, particularly for women, entry into a religious order was often the only way to access education and use their God-given gifts in a wider sphere. Therefore, the commitment to celibacy often "was undertaken as part of the life-form rather than the specific charism of the individual".[39] For Hereford, a sister of the Congregation of St Joseph in the USA, "coming into religious life, the vow of celibacy means that our primary life commitment is to the religious life", and the "Bride of Christ imagery no longer speaks to most of those entering religious communities today".[40] It illustrates the subtle difference, to which no judgement is attached, between someone who feels that their primary commitment is to the religious life, as it is expressed in the particular community, or to the person of Christ. It is simply a reality that reasons to enter religious life vary greatly. I have met a good number of people who, after leaving a religious community, did not feel the desire to sustain their commitment to celibacy, as their primary motivation to seek out life as a religious had never been about that. A male religious I spoke with told me that most of the monks in the congregation with whom he has lived for fifty years had entered monastic life because of a desire for community, discipleship and mission, rather than wanting to choose the celibate life.

The landscape of Christian communities and ministries in the last few decades has changed and vastly widened, including the emergence of the "new monastic" movement. This has made it even clearer that, indeed, there is no intrinsic link between community, ministry and celibacy. Could this be one of the reasons why traditional religious orders in the West no longer attract substantial numbers of younger people? I believe the declining interest in traditional religious life and the surge of new expressions of community and monastic life could be an opportunity to unearth the most ancient of meanings for the charism of consecrated celibacy: wanting to give one's whole life to God in that way simply out of love, without any particular consideration of ministry or community. Whilst service and connection to others are vital components in our walk with God as consecrated celibates, they do not determine our commitment to God as the primary love-relationship of our lives. It does not matter if the nuptial metaphor is employed or not. It is the discovery that my life is so full and filled with seeking God that there is no space for any other primary relationship to which I want to commit myself.

I have deliberately explored the term "celibacy" rather than "chastity". "Chastity" is part of the traditional evangelical counsels of poverty, chastity and obedience, by which those who make public religious vows want to order their lives. Although chastity is often defined as "purity", and this in turn is interpreted as sexual purity, meaning sexual abstinence, I believe this falls short of the meaning of the word. The German word for chastity is *Keuschheit*, which interestingly derives from the Latin adjective *conscius* (from which the English "conscious" is derived). For me, this denotes a being aware of and having an inner clarity and collectedness with which we interact with the world around us, not being controlled by unregulated impulses or easily giving away to the public what is asking to stay in a protected sphere. If we applied this meaning, chastity is something that all followers of Christ are invited to cultivate in their lives and therefore would not capture what this book is about: the voluntary, free choice of completely giving oneself to God, renouncing the possibility of entering a primary relationship with another human being. Maybe one of the reasons why it is difficult to define what we actually mean by "consecrated celibacy" might be that when staying single for "the sake of the kingdom of God" evolved, marriage was the norm for adults, which in the Western world in the twenty-first century is no longer the case. On the contrary, life-long marriage with one partner, or even monogamy, is no longer considered to be the norm.

If we embrace that at the heart of consecrated celibacy lies a voluntary and intentional self-giving to God, it is a logical next step to acknowledge that those called to it are not necessarily meant to join a traditional religious order or a newly founded community. Nor do they require the "official" stamp of approval from an institution. That is not to say that the person who is called to such a commitment is not well advised to stay connected to the wider Body of Christ, engage in ministry, and practise a certain level of accountability!

At the same time, as the Body of Christ, it is our responsibility to support individuals who have this calling. As those gathered at a marriage ceremony express their endeavour to support the couple, so too we are called to do the same for those who want to commit to celibacy as their chosen state of life. We need to let this charism out of the box into which we have put it. As I mentioned before, my passion and the aim of this book is to encourage a *widening of the circle* to include those who are called to make such a commitment, be it with or without the "official" blessing of any of the institutionalized churches. If we do not draw this circle wide enough, we are at high risk of trying to pressurize someone who finds themselves either on the fringes of, or completely outside, the Church into something which is not for them.

A choice to consecrated celibacy, in my view, is open to a person who has never been married, is divorced or widowed. I emphasize again that such a commitment is not making that person "holier" than he or she who is single, whether/not by choice, whether/not content in that state or whether/not looking for a partner. Consecrated celibacy is a voluntary choice in response to a God-given grace—that is why in 1 Corinthians 7:7 it is called a "gift" (Greek *charisma*, meaning "gift" or "grace"). It is not something that can be earned or achieved.

That also raises the question how this sits with someone who identifies as homosexual in their sexual orientation and comes to the conclusion that a commitment to celibacy is what God wants of them. They want to follow the teaching of the Church and/ or their understanding of scripture that God forbids sexual relations between partners of the same sex. In all likelihood, they will speak about choosing to refrain from sexual genital activity in terms of wanting to commit to celibacy. Earlier in this chapter, I mentioned that the vocation to consecrated celibacy is not primarily what one does or does not do with one's sexuality, but rather it is the outer symbol of the giving of oneself voluntarily to God in love. If consecrated celibacy is a "grace" or a "gift", it seems to me that there needs to be more involved than promising not to behave in a certain way. In other words, I would look for what a person feels drawn to *be* rather than primarily at what they do not want to do. Is there any sense of them being drawn to deepen their relationship with God as part of that calling or does it solely derive from a sense of "obedience to the word" or the teaching of the Church? Refraining from sexual activity with a same-sex partner because of one's understanding of scripture does not necessitate a life-long, vowed commitment to consecrated celibacy. This takes us to the question how a call to consecrated celibacy might be discerned and what needs to be considered in the process.

Before that, however, I want to briefly explain why I am working with the terminology of *consecrated* celibacy. I have found Gerald May's description to be the most helpful:

> Consecration is defined as dedication to a divinity. The word comes from the Latin roots *com*, 'with' and *sacer*, 'sacred'. It implies intentionally participating with the divine. We can be dedicated to anything: to a task, a cause, a nation. But we can be consecrated only to God. Consecration means consciously participating in love, intentionally opening ourselves to accept the divinely given gift.[41]

What a beautiful way of describing consecration! We are all invited to participate and open ourselves up to the gift of God's love. The consecrated celibate is participating in this process as a person who voluntarily chooses and promises to permanently remain unmarried, motivated to do so by the love of God. It comes out of a realization that he or she can best participate, as one who has given their self in a total way, to the love experienced in a very personal and exclusive relationship. This is the emphasis, and it is not on achieving moral virtue or being able to *do* more for God.

4

Being called to consecrated celibacy?

Supporting someone who is trying to discern if they are called to consecrated celibacy is not about making them "jump through hoops". Rather, the support should aim to help the person to make as clear a decision as possible whether this way of living would enable them to live their life to the full. Making such a commitment is as significant as a decision to marry. I would like to think that one takes time, considers carefully, prays, tests and talks with others before making a commitment to the state to which one is called. Having said this, I sometimes wonder whether as much care and consideration is applied to the decision to marry as is recommended for someone who commits to consecrated celibacy. Has it, perhaps, in our communities and churches, become far too easy to take that step, because it is thought to be the "default" position for *Christians*? Particularly in denominations where there is an emphasis on sexual abstinence before marriage, many couples feel a pressure to marry quickly so they can enjoy expressing their genital sexuality with each other. Relational aspects and the testing of maturity between partners can easily fall by the wayside.

I would like to explore both the process and some of the content of discernment and formation for someone who wishes to make a vow of consecrated celibacy. When wanting to assist someone in discerning such a calling, it is helpful to agree on a shared understanding of what *discernment* means. Schneiders suggests that, "when it bears upon vocation, discernment is a process of coming to an informed decision before God of what I should do here and now. First, it is a process. It is not an impulse, an infatuation, or a conclusion one jumps to."[42] The emphasis on this being a process helps us to find out whether there is something solid behind our initial excitement when we first seem to hear the call to consecrated celibacy. For others, who might feel scared at the prospect or consider this to be a logical conclusion because of their beliefs, it creates the space and time to excavate what lies at the core of their heart. In traditional religious orders this process of discernment takes significant time, normally a few years (with a maximum of nine years), and involves a great deal of "exploring, testing, studying, praying, discussing, and experimenting before she or he makes a definitive commitment".[43]

Whilst I am not suggesting that the discernment and formation process regarding a vocation to vowed, consecrated celibacy outside a traditional order necessarily needs to be a process of many years, I fully agree that exploration, testing, praying and discussion are vital components of such a process, before a (public) commitment is made. The individual's history, their relationship with God in the past and how this is lived out in the "here and now" of their daily lives, at their place in the Body of Christ, their understanding of what such a commitment entails and requires, and the person's psychological stability, are all important aspects to consider, when exploring a call to this state of life.

Identifying and responding to a vocation is a process of coming to an *informed* decision: "Informed takes in a great deal. It must include, to the best of one's knowledge, everything relevant to the decision that can be investigated in a reasonable span of time."[44] The process of coming to an informed decision is frequently called "formation". Whilst God is the caller and ultimately the One who "forms" us, we cannot walk through this period of formation in isolation. The crucial question for many is who they should turn to for such a process, particularly when exploring a call to consecrated celibacy *outside* a religious order. It can prove challenging to find a suitable person who is willing to fulfil this role and who feels sufficiently equipped for accompanying someone on this journey of discernment and formation. From my experience over the years, this can be said both for people living their faith on the edge of the Church and for those who are settled within church structures. I think that in principle a robustly trained spiritual director is well suited to support an individual in this exploration. Having said this, many spiritual directors might not have come across such a vocation before and might struggle to help the directee to identify and articulate their calling. I know that some people have been quickly referred to a different spiritual director who is a religious or has some experience of religious life. Religious, in turn, however, might find it difficult to imagine how someone could be called to and live a commitment to consecrated celibacy without entering a religious community, or at least a recognized pathway such as the Catholic OCV or the Anglican SCL, which I introduced earlier in Chapter 2. A spiritual director could be tempted to suggest a traditional community or perhaps would not dare to explore with the directee whether making a public vow could be an integral and vital aspect of their journey. I can well imagine that the spiritual director could have questions such as: "What could a commitment to celibacy for this individual look like and who would be 'allowed' to give an 'official blessing'? Might someone overstep a line and get into difficulty in supporting a seeker on this path, without the involvement of clergy?"

One woman who increasingly felt drawn to a deeper life of prayer and relationship with God, and ultimately gave her life to God as a consecrated celibate, put her experience like this:

From there to here, from then to now with the benefit of hindsight, I have truly been finding out who I am. By that I mean, searching for what lives at the heart of me and what is it that I want to give my attention to and place my energies in. I believe I have been trying to get here for at least two decades.

I have spent many more decades trying to fit into the different parish churches I have belonged to. Each one gave to me their community energy and grace and I had good and helpful teaching. However, there came a time when I needed help to understand why parish life was no longer the focus of my attention. I had no desire for any of the vocations or ministries that we can feel drawn to in our Christian living and experience. This time was an enormous hidden journey of struggle and loneliness as I did not have the language or understanding to arrive at any conclusion.

I would be surprised if this experience is an isolated occurrence. It seems to me that a calling to consecrated celibacy, especially in the second half of life, is frequently accompanied by a strong desire for silent prayer and a more contemplative approach to life, both of which ultimately beckon us into a deeper relationship with God. In many parishes, this stance is not readily in view, and there can be a tendency to see people through the lens of roles that need to be occupied and tasks that need to be fulfilled. The idea that God calls people out of parish life into solitude and prayer goes against the grain of our success-orientated culture which all too often can also be found in churches. A spiritual director who is removed from our immediate environment, and who understands what lies at the core of a calling to celibacy, can prove to be an essential gift in identifying a vocation to such a calling. They can ask us the right questions and listen deeply to our experience of our relationship with God.[45]

When I heard God's renewed invitation to consecrated celibacy, I count myself very blessed that the spiritual director I journeyed with at the time had a background of religious life but held my journey in a generous attitude and saw beyond the confines of institutional Church. She helped me to *name* and *understand* God's invitation towards a new level of communion and reciprocal relationship and to respond to this in love. In the months which followed, my spiritual director enabled me to deepen this movement of God's Spirit in my heart, and to discover more deeply what it meant in my search for connection and community in the wider Body of Christ. Additionally, she did not hesitate to ask me some challenging questions when she felt led to do so, for example, before I made my public vow.

At the heart of a period of formation for consecrated celibacy lies the *enabling of inner freedom* for the one who is seeking to discern his or her vocation. The process aims to aid the person's discovery as to whether making such a commitment would deepen their joy in following Christ. Would it allow them to grow ever more deeply into the person they are meant to be and help them to express and use their God-given talents freely? A contemporary translation of the third part of St Ignatius' "Principle and Foundation" of the Thirty-day Spiritual Exercises, sums up very aptly what I am talking about here: "God, let me want and choose what better allows you to deepen your life in me."[46]

For someone who feels invited to consecrated celibacy whilst continuing to work, remaining in their own home or in a home shared with others, many topics which arise for someone contemplating joining a religious order are not relevant or applicable. Such matters include relinquishment of possessions and professional occupation; submission to hierarchical structures, and adopting the features and charisms of the particular congregation. In situations where the person called to celibacy is testing a vocation to, or is already a member of, a community, questions will arise as to how the two vocations can be "knitted together". I believe those questions are relevant whether someone is a member of a new monastic community or any other type of community. Conversations with the leadership team of the community can be instrumental in the provision of a sufficiently robust framework to support the individual's vocation.

Undoubtedly, a decision to commit to consecrated celibacy will impact on our relationship with possessions, career, our friends and family, and our call to serve the world. I would expect that each and every aspect of one's life would be viewed in a new light once such a decision is made. Even if not automatically, it will ultimately lead to life changes. What then are some of the relevant considerations before a person commits themselves to consecrated celibacy?

First, there needs to be a call, which implies that there is a caller. How has the idea that one is called to make such a commitment come about? *How* has the person "heard" this call to give her or his whole being to Christ in this particular way? When? Did it come as a surprise or has a confidence about this vocation quietly grown over the years? Or is it a combination of both? Can the person trace back the beginnings of a sense of being called? What was their reaction to feeling invited to make such a choice? Has the person ever met consecrated celibates, and what are his or her thoughts and fantasies about this state of life? What about their desire to have children? Has the person ever pondered entering a religious order? What is and has been their relationship to the Divine, and, in particular, to the person of Christ? For me, one very important nuance in the discernment for a calling to consecrated celibacy is whether the person can sense that she or he has a choice. Could she or he say "No", and be aware that in so doing this would not diminish God's love for her or him?

As the process of discernment and formation continues, it will become evident whether the person's sense of joy and freedom increases in light of this perceived calling, or whether there is doubt, stress and a draining of energy.

Secondly, it is helpful for the person to have developed a good level of insight and awareness of their own psychological, spiritual, emotional, physical and social wellbeing in life. By this I mean an awareness and understanding of how our upbringing and the wounding we have experienced in our family of origin, how our significant relationships, sexual experiences, and sexual orientation all have an impact on a commitment to celibacy. More obvious issues such as addiction, debilitating and/or chronic health problems, including mental health conditions, need to be addressed during a period of formation. As Schneiders puts it, "the 'I' who is discerning a vocation needs to be lucid and relatively healthy if a good decision to proceed into Religious Life is to be freely made".[47]

Assessing the lucidity and relative healthiness of anyone who senses a calling to celibacy involves asking how the person manages in their daily life, whether he or she is engaged in regular work or has employment, and the types and lengths of significant friendships or relationships.

This is not about meeting some imagined "ideal". We all carry our particular wounds and have our individual struggles. We will always be given opportunities to continue to heal and grow, but we need to ask whether we have a sufficiently healthy insight, psychologically and spiritually, to come to a decision in as much freedom as possible. We need to question to what extent choosing this way of life stems from a need or an attempt to *avoid* facing and dealing with our own issues. There can be fear that no one would *want* to marry us, fear of exploring one's sexual identity, fear of entering any or yet another damaging relationship. A particular wound of which we have to be aware is the trauma of childhood sexual abuse, simply because of its prevalence. Sadly, it is now estimated that one in four or even one in three women, and one in five or one in six men have suffered sexual abuse in their childhood.[48] Trauma of that magnitude will inevitably play a role in choices about our state of life.

Having said all this, we all will have (had) mixed motives when it comes to deciding about celibacy or marriage or, indeed, any other vocation. For example, no married person would honestly deny that, at least to some degree, considerations other than selfless love for the future spouse were involved in the decision to marry. It may have been concerns about financial security, a need to escape the parental home, feeling flattered by being wanted, fear of loneliness or being "left on the shelf", wanting children ... You may have your own particular considerations to add. Similarly, for some who have chosen to enter religious life, not having to worry about finances, employment or avoiding dealing with relational issues might have contributed to their decision. I mention this to emphasize how God can and always *does* work with our mixed motives. That is not a problem for her. The level at which we have looked at our own life, our inner landscape, our sexuality, how we relate to others, and how we can speak about this, will give an indication as to the origins of our desire to commit to Christ as a consecrated celibate.

In all likelihood, the entrance point will be different for men and women and also depend on their sexual orientation. Our self-images and the related God-images we work with, both consciously and unconsciously, deeply influence how we relate to God and respond to a calling to a deeper commitment.

For me, it is about approaching the discernment with as much openness, honesty and humility as I can give in the process. A vocation of this significance and nature needs help in the "here and now", both from God in prayer and from a trusted, respected and mature companion. We need someone who knows us, can challenge our motives, query and probe them and point out the obvious, because we all have blind spots. When it comes to the discernment of a vocation to consecrated celibacy, I feel strongly that it is vital to include in that process at least one person who understands this vocation and in some depth.

I can say from my own experience that when I responded to a perceived calling to consecrated celibacy and entered a community back in 1986, my motivation was not purely my love for Christ: I was afraid of marriage as my parents were divorced and I had never experienced a happy family life. There was the unsaid hope that a community of celibate women would give me the motherly love I had missed out on. After four years of living more deeply into the calling, moving towards the completion of my studies, continuing to have a sense of God confirming this vocation, these motives only came to the fore following the community's refusal to allow me to join them. As painful as this was, God used the situation to unearth some of these fears and hurts and brought about some healing. When the invitation to consecrated celibacy, unmistakable yet unbidden, surfaced for me again twenty years later, I was by then a more whole and mature person. I had dealt with a lot more of my wounds and become more familiar with my inner landscape. Through nearly two decades, I had shared a house and lived in intentional Christian community, I had sought ongoing spiritual accompaniment and undergone two years of therapy after a burnout. Yet even then, when moving towards a public profession of that commitment, my spiritual director and I looked closely at my motivations for making a lifelong commitment to celibacy. I undertook further testing and praying, reflected deeply on the wording of my vow, and explored how my calling to consecrated celibacy could be "knitted more closely together" with my novitiate in the Northumbria Community. The longer I live into my commitment, the more I can see why God prevented me joining a religious community. It would have not been lifegiving for me but would have restricted my growth to greater freedom. I also become aware of the different layers in my own heart which all played and continue to play their part in my vocation. And every time I discover something else about myself and God, once more God invites me to live more deeply into the covenant with the Beloved. I know from friends who are married that exactly the same applies to their relationship with their spouse. We never arrive or are settled "once and for all". Formation is a life-long process, and a requirement for sustaining any long-term relationship if we want it to remain fresh and alive. At times, it can be excruciatingly painful to stay in that relationship. We would rather run away than continue working at it. As I mentioned earlier, no matter which state of life we find ourselves in, there will always be challenges. We need to find our own way of dealing with them and of responding to the inner workings of God in our unique life context.

I have shared some of the details of my own journey into consecrated celibacy to make the point that God works in, with and through our brokenness. In fact, often it can be precisely our brokenness that God uses to ignite a deep search and desire for him. At the same time, we need to be realistic and honest about our struggles, capabilities and motives, for only then can we come to a choice made in as much freedom as possible at a point in time.

Vital components of (ongoing) formation and discernment are, in my view, a commitment to cultivate a deep prayer life, engagement and sufficient grounding in scripture, a personal relationship with Christ, continued inner work in the cell of our own hearts where we discover our shadow and the love of God, spiritual direction and some exposure to and involvement with the wider Body of Christ.

The latter brings me to the *third* consideration when contemplating a call to consecrated celibacy. Even if we no longer consider the institutional Church as our "spiritual home", we cannot walk this path in isolation. A calling to consecrated celibacy has to be grounded. *We* have to be grounded in our being, in living our life, and in relating to God, to others and to the world. Otherwise we easily risk walking with our "head in the clouds", with a spirituality and life that have no connection with the real world. Particularly when we live by ourselves, we can quickly slide into the illusion of how spiritual and holy we have become. That is, until we have an encounter with a real person, who quickly brings us "down to earth" and in contact with our flaws, faults and limitations once again. That is precisely why we need to have some of these encounters intentionally built into our life and a space to reflect on ourselves in the presence of a compassionate listener. A quote from Paul Schütz expresses what I want to say: "In truth, our neighbour is not in our way, but he stands on the edge of the abyss as a guardian angel who prevents us from drifting away from the realities of life into illusion."[49] There is a saying amongst religious communities that no one should be allowed to live alone unless they have gone through the fire of fellowship. I can certainly testify that I have learnt a lot about myself whilst living with others in community. I was regularly confronted with my reactions and sensitivities. Community living led me to reflect about myself, sometimes only after hearing how others had experienced me. I was led to make petition to God for his patience, humility and for his love to be worked out in me, in my continued experience of living closely with others. This was quite humiliating at times and hard work, but I am very grateful now to have had this "rubbing off" in community. Just in case you wonder, I am in no way saying that I am a finished product! I continue to need the mirroring and feedback of trusted friends as my guardian angels. Living on my own also continues to teach me very valuable lessons.

Fourthly, I believe it is important to consider who and what will provide us with sufficient support to live out a commitment to consecrated celibacy "in the world", or, more precisely, in *our* place in the world, to which God has called us. Female Catholics who feel drawn to consecrated celibacy will almost certainly consider the rite reserved for consecrated virgins. They would thus become part of the "Order of the Consecrated Virgins" (OCV). Both male and female Anglicans have the option to join the "Single Consecrated Life" (SCL).[50] I imagine that joining any of these dispersed "communities" brings with it an "official recognition" of one's state of life. It puts one into a context and enables connections with others who have made the same commitment. Both the OCV and SCL organize annual gatherings.

With regard to my own journey, I have looked into both the OCV and SCL before and after making my public vow. As I have no roots in the Anglican Church, the SCL did not seem right for me, and although I had been baptized and confirmed in the Catholic Church, my connections at that time were non-existent. But even after I returned to the Catholic Church years later (albeit still on the edges!) and wondered again whether the OCV might be an additional place to hold my vocation, this did not resonate with me.

Prior to making my public commitment, which was shortly after the start of my novitiate with the Northumbria Community, I queried whether the Community and our rule of life would provide a sufficiently strong framework to support my particular calling to consecrated celibacy. I noticed within me a desire for an "official recognition" of my state of life. I had often thought that I would like to have either two or three letters after my name as do religious, e.g. "SJ", indicating Jesuits ("Society of Jesus"), or "OSB" for a Benedictine monk or nun. Or alternatively, at least a "Sr" in front of my name. Anyone dealing with such religious will immediately recognize who they are and the order they belong to. Eventually, though, I felt led by God to accept that whilst living as a consecrated celibate is indeed at the core of who I am, this was not something for me to "show" explicitly or to be recognized in me through a "title". Rather, I felt invited to live out this calling in (relative) obscurity, letting it be enough for me that God and a few close friends, together with my spiritual director, know the meaning and importance of my self-gift to him. It felt that God with a smile on her face reminded me that Jesus did not have three letters after his name, nor did he have any "official" recognition of staying single by the religious institutions of his time. If anything, he was probably mocked for his celibacy, because as described earlier, to the practising Jew of that day not marrying was an offence to God. I also remembered that after the door to the community of sisters closed in the early 1990s, I heard God say to me that he did not want me to attach my heart too closely to a vocation. This made me realize again that anything in our lives has the potential to become more important than God, even a vocation or a state of life!

Whilst the commitment to consecrated celibacy expresses the desire for a deep seeking of God which is made possible by the giving of oneself, we are all invited to order and focus our "loves" for the sake of God's love. It is for a reason that Jesus reminds us that loving God is the *first* commandment. We are all in need of ordering our desires. When this happens over a lifetime, our relationship with God, ourselves, others, our belongings and creation begins to fall into place, and we enter a freedom which is not possible to attain otherwise. Such an approach to consecrated celibacy, and indeed to life in general, does not put an emphasis on *ascetism*, where we seek to achieve "spiritual things" by *renouncing* things such as possessions, pleasures and sexual intimacy. Rather, we aim to be caught up in a greater love, which enables us *to let go*. A shift towards letting go rather than renouncement also helps us to avoid being caught in an unhelpful dualism of sexual repression/libertinism, as Sarah Coakley suggests in her book *The New Asceticism*.[51] Cynthia Bourgeault puts it this way: "There is slight but crucial difference in flavour between renunciation and letting go" where we preserve our chastity by not clinging.[52] For me, the difference lies in the notion that when we renounce, *we are still in control*, whereas when we let go, *we surrender to Another*.

To me, this would explain, perhaps, why Paul put into the centre of his explorations of the married and single life this exhortation:

> From now on those who have wives should live as if they do not; those who mourn, as if they did not; those who are happy, as if they were not; those who buy something, as if it were not theirs to keep; those who use the things of the world, as if not engrossed in them. For this world in its present form is passing away. (1 Corinthians 7:29–31)

Have you ever asked yourself how these three verses ended up in this chapter? I wonder whether it is about holding lightly *any* vocation, *any* charism, *any* state of life, *anything* we do (especially those things we "do for God"!) and becoming "single" "in the sense of mind and heart both going in the same direction, aligned with God, wanting one thing only".[53] Ignatius of Loyola called this "indifference" towards the circumstances in our life. We learn to receive and share everything happily with Christ and are equally happy to give away. We grow in freedom to attain and yield to love as the ultimate goal of our lives.

I am wearing a ring (as many other consecrated celibates I know do) as an outward expression of my commitment. This can be a signal to anyone who might become "interested" in me that I am not available. When asked about my ring, I give varying answers, depending on the person and context when the question arises! I take great encouragement from something Richard Rohr said to me when I shared with him my commitment:

> I think it might just be single people like you who resurrect a purer meaning to chosen celibacy. Religious life, as presently lived, just has too many securities, perks, and pay offs which compromises the message and the choice.[54]

5

Sexuality and celibacy

Or: How, then, do we live as consecrated celibates?

At this point, I would like to expand on the theme of sexuality. Our unique expression of sexuality is deeply influenced and formed from our earliest childhood onwards. Our upbringing and relatedness determines to a great deal how *we* relate—to anything. Exploring and choosing consecrated celibacy is not about ignoring or not engaging with our sexuality. Quite the contrary. How we understand, embrace and live with our own sexuality is of great importance in discerning a call to committed celibacy as well as living and being able to sustain this vocation wholeheartedly and with integrity. I therefore want to give this exploration the space I feel it deserves. Our starting point, I believe, has to be one of *respect* and *regard* towards our sexuality. Interestingly, both words denote a "guarding", "showing concern for" and "looking again". And that is what I want to do here: Look and *look again.*

Obviously sexuality is a huge theme. We often tend to think about it in terms of genital sexuality only. But it is about so much more. It includes our whole person, body, gender, identity, how we relate to ourselves, to others, to creation, to God. Sexuality is fundamental to our being human. It is our life force, the creative energy in our being that propels us towards connection with others, that sits in our desire to bring forth life, to nurture and care, to give form and shape. Being human means to be sexual—and spiritual. Both include body, mind and spirit. We have no choice about being sexual. The same applies to being spiritual. We might not acknowledge or realize it, but it is what makes us human. And the two are inseparably linked in our "being". Rob Bell beautifully expresses this in a more lyrical approach at the beginning of his book *Sex God*:

> *This* is actually about *that*.
> Whether it's what we do with our energies
> or how we feel about our bodies
> or wanting to have the control in relationships
> or trying to recover from heartbreak
> or dealing with our ferocious appetites
> or the difficulty of communicating
>   clearly with those we love
> or longing for something or someone better,
> much of life is in some way connected
>   with our sexuality.

And when we begin to sort through all of
    the issues surrounding our sexuality,
    we quickly end up in the spiritual,
because this
    is always about that. . . .
It's always about something else.
Something deeper. Something behind it all.
You can't talk about sexuality without talking
    about how we were made. And that will
    inevitably lead you to who made us. At
    some point you have to talk about God.
Sex. God. They are connected. And they can't
    be separated. Where the one is, you will
    always find the other. . . . Sexuality is the 'this'
    and spirituality is the 'that'. To make sense
    of the one, we have to explore the other.[55]

These are powerful statements. Sexuality and spirituality are two facets of the jewel of our unique, human expression of the Divine. *We* are this jewel. To make sense of ourselves, we have to explore both our spirituality and our sexuality. Just think of the implications of that statement for a moment, particularly for those of us who have chosen celibacy as the defining part of our God-quest. Another reason I emphasize this is that the Church as a whole has failed to do justice to this connection. On the contrary, from her earliest history, the Church has anxiously tried to separate the two. This dualistic split between the "spiritual" and the "physical", or the "immortal soul" and the "physical body", was heavily influenced by Greek philosophy, in particular by Plato. Add to this backdrop the Old Testament's purity laws, and you have a perfect environment for generating the approach of the Christian Church, in its first few hundred years of existence, that "spiritual things" were "pure", and anything to do with the body "unclean", and eventually "sinful". For the early Church Fathers, it was then a logical step to assume that sexual abstinence was to be practised in order to achieve "purity for the soul". As I indicated in the chapter about the history of consecrated celibacy, from the earliest times, male celibacy in particular was seen predominantly as an ascetic way. Sexuality was both supressed and repressed, for the sake of gaining "a higher good". And because the body was considered the source of sexual dangers, those who embarked on controlling their sexual drives through staying genitally abstinent soon claimed that this was the "holier" way. It is quite sobering and sad to read *how* negative the Church Fathers' view of the body and sexuality was, and to realize that "in the subsequent centuries, although modifications took place, the basic negativity never gave up its relentless grip".[56] As far as I am concerned, we still have not fully recovered from that.

What riches we could offer "to the world" if we taught about the *meaning* of sex and our being sexual in our churches and communities! That *this* is about *that*. That sexuality is an expression of our spirituality, that it is inherently good, and we do not need to fear or banish it. That sexuality expresses itself in a myriad of ways and is part of our being created in God's image. Whilst the Church might theoretically affirm this positive approach in some places, the practice and reality often reflect the opposite. Have you ever heard a sermon about the goodness of sexuality in all of us? And I am not talking about a wedding ceremony where sexuality is praised exclusively for those who are married and reduced to the physical coming together of a couple. I agree with Wunnibald Müller, a German psychotherapist practising in a Benedictine monastery, who believes that it is mainly the mystical streams in the Church that expressed a more positive view of human sexuality. They see sexuality as a positive force and honour sexuality as the source of spirituality. The mystics emphasize how important it is to have "Eros and sexuality for a relationship to God which is alive. They make us aware that there is a transcendent potential in sexuality which wants to lead us into the experience of the most intimate union with God. They understand sexuality as a force which leads us beyond ourselves, which beckons us to empty ourselves, forget ourselves, and to unify."[57] Their unashamed use of erotic language to describe their experiences with the Divine opens for us a door into this connection between sexuality and spirituality.

It is precisely because of the transcendent potential in our sexuality that we all need to work out which language, images, symbols and metaphors speak to us in a helpful way about the God we seek. What is it that helps us to take our deepest desires into prayer? What *are* our deepest desires (they are not what our ego craves)? What makes us feel alive and what drains our energy? How do we nurture others? How do we express our creative energy? What opens us towards the Holy, and what makes us close down? Do we employ male or female "God-language", do we speak of "Father", or "Mother", or "Sophia", or "Spirit"? Gender, our self-image and God-image, inevitably play a crucial role in how much we allow ourselves to expand our ways of relating to God. Janet Ruffing, in her book *Spiritual Direction: Beyond the Beginnings*, stresses how important it is that a spiritual director identifies "particular Jesus- or God-images that can comfortably carry a directee's erotic energies. These energies are the human, instinctual root of our insatiable desire for the Other, who is ultimately God. If we do not integrate these erotic longings in our prayer, we may diminish our capacity for entering into this intimacy with God."[58] Our erotic desires are to inform our prayer and our prayer is to direct our desires for intimacy, belonging and generativity. Because *this* is about *that*.

The Church as a whole still remains silent on sexuality, its place in our lives and in regard to its role in the wholeness of our relationship with God. I believe this applies to Anglican, Catholic and any of the mainstream evangelical churches. What we tend to hear is that singleness means getting prepared for marriage, sex is only for marriage, and what kind of behaviour in relation to sex is *not* allowed and is sinful. In her book on singleness, Kate Wharton, an Anglican priest and now a committed celibate, shares the example of how teenagers were desperate to talk to their youth leaders about sex and sexuality but were denied the opportunity. Think about your own church or community, and ask whether it is any different? We find it so difficult to create safe and appropriate spaces for people to go deeper in their exploration. We do not make the crucial connection between sexuality and spirituality, but rather perpetuate the disconnection. I would also ask whether it is precisely this disconnection that has contributed to the many sad cases where the Church apparently held an explicit, exterior moral code, whilst knowing that her own clergy sexually, physically and emotionally abused hundreds, even thousands of people in their care. Codes of ethics and statements on moral behaviour are insufficient. The failure to model such statements further deepens the shame which is associated with anything relating to our bodies and sexuality. Society, whilst applying a different world view, does the same: The outer appearance of our bodies is what counts. More often than not our understanding of sexuality is reduced to genital activity. We are led to believe that we can do anything we like, that engaging sexually with each other is of no consequence inwardly. The split between our body and our soul continues, despite a "freer" approach to sex. A sex therapist once said to me that being "shameless" is just another way of trying to avoid dealing with the shame we feel, by "acting out". Neither Church nor society encourage us to ask questions and to have a closer look at ourselves and what sexuality and our sexual behaviour *means*, or where it comes from. Whenever we dare to challenge either position, we are often viewed as too liberal in church, or as being "phobic" of something or someone in society. None of this is helpful. If our feelings and thoughts are immediately met with opinions and answers delivered through a lens of what is perceived to be "politically correct" on the one hand or "biblical" on the other, this will only hinder us in an honest exploration of our truest self, and the discovery our deepest desires. And this exploration takes time. An example of this search might result in some people finally embracing their same-sex attraction. Others, in experiencing a dissonance within themselves, might want to seek the professional help of a therapist in exploring more deeply how their own experience of sexuality, and maybe sexual or other forms of abuse in their lives, has impacted on their expression of sexuality. All individuals should have the freedom to find out and talk about their sexuality, with an exploration that is allowed to move in any direction.

Why am I mentioning all of this? Because if we are to explore our sexuality as consecrated celibates, we are not embarking on this journey in a vacuum. How we see ourselves, and how deeply we dare to delve into the themes surrounding our sexuality and relationship with God, inevitably will be influenced by the culture in which we live, and how this is manifest in the different spheres of our life, family and friends, church and society. A good starting point might be to take stock and look at how our experiences in life have shaped our attitude towards sexuality. Questions we can ask are: how have we experienced sex and sexuality in our life, beginning with our family of origin? Was there ever open talk about it? Did our parents or parental figures display affection and tenderness—with each other, with us and our siblings? Or was there a shame-filled silence around anything to do with sex? Was there abuse and violence? What was the attitude towards the body, *my* body? How did I experience my own gender and what were the messages I heard? What was I told is "masculine" and what is "feminine"? You can use these questions and apply them to your experiences at school, to your peer relations, your relationship with authority, at university, at work . . . Further questions to explore sexuality are linked to creativity and generativity: How do I express creativity in my life? What about my desire to have children? What does "being fruitful" mean to me? How could I live this as a consecrated celibate? What legacy do I want to leave behind in this world? Which activities in my life help me to express nurture and care towards myself and others? How and where do I experience pleasure? What does God feel about me having pleasure? How do I approach work and rest?

Can I rest? Pondering these kinds of questions will help you to open up this terrain and see where you are at, currently. More can be found at the end of this book.

I hope that your starting point, at least intellectually, can be that fundamentally, sexuality is good. Earlier in this book, we looked at the creation story in Genesis where God called everything s/he made "good" and "very good". However, mentally agreeing with something is, as we all know, not the same as experiencing and living it. In all likelihood, we all experience a discrepancy between the two. But somehow to trust that God did not make a mistake when s/he created us as needy creatures is not a bad place to begin a deeper exploration of what is a fundamental part of being human. Having needs means to be needy, and that is why I deliberately chose to use this term. If you are like me, it easily evokes a reaction within, which lets us know that "needy" is not how we would like to see ourselves or be perceived by others. But remember, Jesus came into this world as a needy baby, too. He needed to be fed, cleaned, held and taught. He also had to work out for himself who he was, who God was, and what it meant to be human.

I believe that the Church's teaching about sexuality has been deeply influenced by the fall/redemption framework which put an emphasis on "original sin", instead of "original blessing" and the goodness of God's creation which we have been tasked to care for, and, as I mentioned in Chapter 1, to be co-creators with God. Were we to start from a state of being blessed, rather than "having fallen", then celebrating pleasure would come more naturally to us. As Matthew Fox points out: "If creation is a blessing and a constantly original one, then our proper response would be to enjoy it. Pleasure is one of the deepest spiritual experiences of our lives." He continues: "If we savored more, we would buy less. We would be less compulsive, less unsatisfied. We would also work less and play more, and thus open up work opportunities to the many unemployed and underemployed in our culture. If we savored more we would communicate more deeply, relate more fully, compete less regularly, and celebrate more authentically. We would be relating more deeply to ourselves, to creation in all its blessedness, to history past and future, to the Now and to God."[59]

Here is a hint that sexuality, more than anything else, is about *connection,* and how we connect. And so is spirituality. And this is what I would like to explore next. *We are born this way.* From the moment of our conception, what we will become silently nestles and grows in our mother's womb. We are completely inside another human being, we are separate, *and* we are in total union. This sharing of life in the womb of our mother is the deepest bodily connection we will ever experience in this life, even if it is beyond our consciousness.

And then, our visible entrance into this world starts with a big disconnection. We are pressed and pushed out of a warm, protective space and visibly become a separate person, crying to return to the place we had to leave. Yet it takes a couple of years of development until we realize that we are indeed a separate being. We discover our "self" for the first time—but we can only do so in relationship. As Martin Buber put it: it is a "Thou" who tells me that I am. We cannot develop without being separate or without being connected.

This starting point is a tension and the paradox at the core of our human existence. Ultimately, what makes us unique is our essential aloneness. And it is from that place of aloneness that we want and need to connect with what is *not* us. We strive for union, where our sense of self is maintained yet fused with another. And the ultimate "Other" is God. We might not be aware of it, but in all our seeking, the search for the Divine is present, our need for connection with the source of all things. Christine Valters Paintner put it like this:

> Sexuality and the erotic are fundamental urges we have as human beings to move us beyond our solipsistic, preoccupied selves into a world of community and connection. (. . .) What if our call is to make love to life itself, whether or not we express it in a physically intimate way with another person? What if this sexual desire were about tapping into a source of energy that awakens us to our deepest longing for connection?[60]

Brene Brown, a social researcher, distils this further, in saying that "Connection is why we're here. We are hardwired to connect with others, it's what gives purpose and meaning to our lives, and without it there is suffering."[61] As I explored earlier, our desire for connection with "the other" ultimately includes and is aimed at God. That necessarily means that whenever we lose sight of our connection with the Divine, we are missing something vital. But, once again, the opposite is true just as much, and is particularly important for us to note in the context of consecrated celibacy. Whenever we think we have no need to connect with other human beings on a deep level, we not only miss something crucial but actually run the risk of becoming increasingly unable to connect in empathy or intimacy, or, at worst, eventually develop dysfunctional, or even harmful ways of relating to those around us.

To understand connection, we need to explore intimacy. I believe that *intimacy* is one of the most important aspects of our sexuality. Without it, people might be very active for God, have many friendships, or even sexual relationships, but will not necessarily nor automatically experience meaningful connection. For the committed celibate, his or her ability to form intimate relationships, without seeking genital sexual encounters, is a key requirement to enter and sustain that state of life. It forms the basis for the giving of oneself in openness, care and devotion to others.

"Intimacy is always personal. It is the fusing and the counterpointing of personalities. Everyone needs intimacy. Everyone craves it. But intimacy is not found; it doesn't just happen. The dynamics by which interpersonal intimacy is allowed to arise are self-awareness and self-disclosure in the hearing of another."[62] What Clark, a Capuchin, says here, applies to intimacy in all of our relationships, including the one with God, ourselves and with anything created. As consecrated celibates we have made our relationship to God the focal point of our life whilst laying aside the physical genital relationship with another. But we will only get to know God more intimately to the degree that we are willing to get to know ourselves. Self-knowledge and God-knowledge always go together and only increase in tandem-like fashion. "The search for God and the search for our True Self finally are the same search."[63]

Increasing our self-knowledge as the basis for intimacy is a vital movement in our lives. It is a paradox, as our ability to form intimate relationships by means of disclosing some of the deeper parts of our inner being requires that we spend time *alone*. We must pause, stop and notice our thoughts and feelings, and the stories we are telling ourselves. We need to meet and befriend our essential aloneness, which we often experience as being lonely, sometimes desperately so. Our first instinct is to find a way of easing that sense of loneliness, because it feels so uncomfortable. Consciously welcoming it might seem counterintuitive and is a practice that requires intention and patience. Over time it will help us to realize that, ultimately, we do indeed walk our own life journey, at its deepest level, completely alone—*with God*. At the core, there is only God and us, and this is the Holy Space where both our True Self and God dwell, and where they are one. Henri Nouwen called this process the "conversion from loneliness into solitude. Instead of running away from our loneliness and trying to forget or deny it, we have to protect it and turn it into a fruitful solitude. To live a spiritual life we must first find the courage to enter into the desert of our loneliness and to change it by gentle and persistent efforts into a garden of solitude."[64]

Learning to welcome our loneliness does not mean that we conceal our need for connection with others or that we never reach out when we feel lonely! I believe the invitation is to discern. There is a time to reach out, maybe meet with someone or pick up the phone and connect, and on the other hand there is the time for a deliberate engagement with our inner world. The more we learn to explore and inhabit our internal deserts, the more we will be able to share of ourselves in ways that are not possessive and can give rise to intimate *moments*. Intimate moments can also arise when we relate to creation, when we really *see* a flower, a tree, a bee, a bird. Or when we engage mindfully in a creative process, be it pottey, baking bread, planting seeds . . . We cannot force such moments to happen, nor can we cling to them. In these moments who or what we are connecting with opens up and we see reality on a deeper level. In relation to other human beings, these moments are more likely to occur when we disclose discoveries we have made about ourselves. This does not have to be in words. Only two per cent of our communication is verbal. Our tears speak volumes when we dare to show them. Holding out a hand, indicating we need someone to hold it, says it all. Comforting a child sitting on our lap connects us beyond words. Silently watching a sunrise together requires no comment. When another lets us know that they hear and see us, something happens on a deep level to us both. It is as if we both glimpse parts of ourselves in new ways and as a result we are both enlarged. This kind of encounter requires us to embrace vulnerability, just as entering into our internal deserts does. We need a vulnerability to show ourselves and to risk being hurt. Without taking this risk, we might stay "safe", but we will not find what we desire most, intimacy and connection. And this applies to our relationships with the human *and* the Divine. Children do this naturally. That is why so much of our spiritual journey, especially in the second half of life, is about un-learning and re-discovering.

There is no intimacy without vulnerability. And this can only occur where we take the risk of uncovering. In other words, where we allow ourselves and someone else to see us, or at least parts of us, *naked*. Can you see the connection again? That *this* is about *that*? That both sexuality and spirituality essentially are about uncovering? We want it, but we fear it at the same time.

"Here's the crux of the struggle: *I want to experience your vulnerability, but I don't want to be vulnerable. Vulnerability is courage in you and inadequacy in me. I'm drawn to your vulnerability but repelled by mine.*"[65]

How true. We are all caught in this crucible which Brene Brown describes in this quote. She started off wanting to find out about "connection" and ended up researching vulnerability and shame. I believe her findings are essential to our understanding of sexuality and intimacy. Sexuality is deeply shame-laden, especially as Christianity historically has put such an emphasis on sexual sin. Brene Brown found that shame is one of the biggest blocks to vulnerability. She defines shame as "the intensely painful feeling or experience of believing that we are flawed and therefore unworthy of love and belonging".[66] It is hidden in and often driven by our sense of "not being . . . enough". Does this sound familiar to you? That you are not doing enough, not trying hard enough? That what you are creating is not worth looking at? That your need to belong, to connect and to be fruitful is unwelcome? That you *are* not enough, *are* not good, and therefore not loveable? Whilst shame is closely linked with abuse and trauma, it is not restricted to victims who have survived such events. We all experience shame in our lives. And, in all likelihood, we find it very difficult to speak about it. That is how shame works and how it grows. Shame keeps us trapped in the dark and often prevents us from setting even the first step into our own, inner desert, or allowing someone else see it. We fear it is too painful. Yet, as we discussed, exploring our inner life is one of the most essential tasks in our spiritual life. It is the things which we keep in the dark that will become the *real* driving forces in our lives, even if we are not aware of them. That was one of Freud's main discoveries. Brene Brown found that both our bodies and sex are amongst the twelve most common "shame categories", next to motherhood/fatherhood, religion, ageing and a few others. That is why we need to become aware of shame in our own lives and where it hides. We cannot resist shame, but only learn to find ways of becoming shame resilient. One of the great antidotes to shame is empathy. For this to happen we need to move what we are ashamed of out of the closet and reach out for help. It is those who *own* and *share* their story, who develop the greatest level of shame resilience. Acknowledging our need for help and admitting that we cannot undertake this journey on our own is therefore, I believe, crucial if we want to continue in our explorations of our sexuality.

We cannot do this looking, and looking again, by ourselves. We need someone to accompany us. This can be a friend, a spiritual director, or a therapist. Whoever they are, they need to be a mature, compassionate "other" who has done enough of their own inner work so that they can hold a safe space for us, free of judgements. We need their empathy and offering of connection to help us in becoming shame resilient. Sometimes that will mean allowing us to realize that whilst we may talk a lot, we are not connecting with our feelings, and that we need help to identify and name our experience. With regards to our sexuality, for many of us, this may be for the first time in our lives. Has anyone grown up with parents who spoke about this freely? Shame can be overcome when we are enabled to connect with our feelings and hear that in them we are not alone. We are heard and we are seen—and we are worthy of being loved. The acceptance by someone else, no matter what we share, helps us gradually to open up and accept ourselves. It is a long journey of becoming increasingly honest with ourselves and to become shame resilient. It will take a lifetime; in fact, it *is* our life. Where we begin to accept what is within ourselves, we can acknowledge it. And with acknowledgement comes the possibility of owning our sexuality, in all its expressions, with all of its irrational elements. This is one of the most important steps required for human sexuality and enables us to channel and moderate it from a place of freedom.[67]

Learning to speak about our sexuality in front of another helps to prevent us from making the choice of celibacy whilst we knowingly deny or suppress our sexuality, or hope to avoid dealing with issues such as trauma, abuse, sexual identity, difficulties relating to others or the impact of previous sexual relationships. Having said this, sometimes, the deepest parts of ourselves which remain unknown to us will only surface *after* we have made a commitment. Here it is our newly found state in life that provides us with the safety and security we need, to allow our awareness to emerge. In any case, it is vital that *we have started* on a journey, in which we are committed to become increasingly free to speak without shame of that powerful life-force within us, which has such huge potential, for good and for bad.

As I already hinted, it is the *unexamined* urges and drives that intimidate us. Clark states that our sexual behaviour only becomes uncontrollable when we ignore or deny our urges, drives and needs, and in particular our need for intimacy: "I don't believe that simply gratifying my urge for physical sex or my drive for romantic involvement will ever satisfy my human need for intimacy. But if I ignore or deny my need for intimacy, I can expect those aspects of myself which are more instinctual to push me with more than usual force. If my biological urge and my bio-psychological drive are simply indulged and gratified in themselves, the activities only become addictive, while the underlying hunger for intimacy remains unmet."[68] To me, that shows that even engaging in genital sexual activity can become a way of *avoiding* vulnerability and intimacy. At its worst, our avoidance can lead to behaviour that seeks to exert power and control over someone else, something that ultimately can lead to abusing others, emotionally, physically or sexually.

That is why we are well advised to gain insight into the triggers that cause our protective mechanisms to kick in. We employ these mechanisms to avoid discomfort. Often, we adopt them early in childhood when we are indeed dependent and vulnerable. But when we inappropriately continue with them into adulthood, they become a hindrance to growth and become ways in which we can avoid being seen and choosing to be vulnerable. Over time, they become part of who we *think* we are, like a seemingly protective, additional layer of skin that attaches itself to our being. We need to bear in mind that these strategies were originally necessary for our survival, particularly if we experienced trauma in our childhood. That is why we get so attached to them. We need to honour them first, before we label or try to get rid of them as "sin". These defences can help to teach us and can point to the original hurts, which ask for our loving attention and compassion and are thus slowly integrated in our adult self. Addiction, or making a "god" out of a defence mechanism is frequently only a small step away, and to some extent we are all addicted, even if it is only to our way of thinking. Addiction and attachment are often linked to an inner resistance and avoidance of looking intentionally at ourselves. It is another reminder of why we need the help of a wise companion:

> Skillful spiritual direction conversations may evoke resistance because they focus attention, raise awareness, and make demands for conversion on the directee. The spiritual direction conversation itself is historically a powerful ascetical tool precisely because it

requires ongoing consciousness and reflection
on the part of the directees.[69]

There are endless layers of skin attached to us. As Eustace
realized in C. S. Lewis' *The Voyage of the Dawn Treader*,
after he had turned into a dragon, no matter how hard
he tried, he could not rid himself of his dragon skin. It
was only when he heard Aslan tell him: "You will have
to let me undress you" that he could be freed. Yes, it is
scary. Yes, it is very painful at times. But what joy when
we, like Eustace, find ourselves thrown into the water
of our own well, and freely splash and swim, more and
more as the persons we are made to be.

The fruit of our labour, the ongoing reflection, and the
gradual ordering of our desires in Love, is priceless. The
process of integrating our sexuality into the wholeness
of our bodily and spiritual being, into our relatedness
in life, will release us into ever greater levels of freedom
and joy. Therefore, let us continue and not give up!

This freedom includes realizing that, whilst we can
live out many aspects of our sexuality in non-genital
ways, our biological urges and drives will make
themselves known at times. There will always remain
something wild and unpredictable about our sexuality.
We will never be in a place where we can say that we have
"mastered" our physiological sensations and instincts.
When we reach that place of recognition, we can find that
it becomes a gateway to our ever-deepening surrender
to God. Our sexuality is not something to be "fixed" or

controlled; instead it beckons us to continue to care for, attend to and befriend all parts of ourselves, especially those which still feel strange and alien. Befriending and welcoming do not imply that we do not have choices or that we are helpless and must simply succumb to our urges and emotions whenever they show up. It is our responsibility to choose behaviours that enable us to honour the commitments we have made in life. This may be evident when it involves choices about genital activity with another person, but perhaps is less clear when it only involves us. The traditional view is that the consecrated celibate is genitally abstinent, and this includes sexual activity with oneself. Whilst the view that it is "dangerous" no longer seems to be the dominant one, many are still concerned that masturbation is sinful and worry that there is "danger" through potential fantasies attached to it. Others see it as pathological or something that is only "normal" during adolescence. The conclusion therefore is, best "not to go there" at all. An attitude like that will not encourage self-exploration nor lead to an increase in self-knowledge. As I said, self-exploration and self-knowledge are vital if we are to grow in our knowledge of God, and our ability to speak about our sexuality. In all likelihood, condemning self-pleasure outright may lead us into supressing awareness of certain aspects of our physicality. And as we have seen before, this will influence our behaviour even more, precisely because we abandoned these aspects or pushed them into our unconscious. Müller states that it is vital to encounter "my sexual feelings, fantasies, physical movements in a way that not only sees them as expressions of genital desire, but I am open to learn something in and through them about what is an essential part of me".[70]

Müller comes to the conclusion that, truthfully, any celibate person, to a greater or lesser extent, will have to deal with the fact of masturbation in life. Müller sees masturbation not as sin or moral failure but also not completely in harmony with committed celibacy. He sees masturbation as an expression of our imperfection, "lacking behind the ideal of celibacy to outgrow the need for genital activity". He also believes that masturbation is not destructive, whereas feelings of guilt about it starts an unhelpful, self-destructive process. He suggests that this is often rooted in feelings of guilt about sexuality as a whole.[71] I wonder whether at the root of this self-destructive process lie not feelings of guilt but rather of *shame*. We not only feel guilty, but deep down we experience emotionally that something fundamentally is wrong with being sexual or having sexual needs. As I said, what we think we believe and our actual belief and experience can be worlds apart.

I wonder whether this suggested ideal of total genital abstinence for a consecrated celibate (or any single person according to the teaching of the Church) is actually helpful. Could it precisely be this ideal that gives rise to the destructive feelings of shame that are connected with our sexuality? Do we simply not dare to think that maybe, just maybe, God might not have a problem with sexual self-pleasure? Before taking this further, I want to draw a large circle around the question of how we are living with our physical urges. This, I believe, will aid us in giving them the respect they deserve. The bigger circle here is our *body* and the theme of *pleasure* which I touched upon earlier.

Scripture reminds us that our "bodies are temples of the Holy Spirit" (1 Corinthians 6:19). Our bodies carry something, someone holy. John O'Donohue wraps these words around this truth:

> The body is a sacrament ... a visible sign of invisible grace ... All our inner life and intimacy of soul longs to find an outer mirror. It longs for a form in which it can be seen, felt, and touched. The body is the mirror where the secret world of the soul comes to expression. The body is a sacred threshold; and it deserves to be respected, minded, and understood in its spiritual nature.[72]

He evokes poetically the mystery of the invitation to our surrender and union with the Divine *with* and *in* our bodies. But this is quite a journey, because, generally speaking, we have managed to cut ourselves off from the experience of *being bodily*. Earlier we explored how a dualistic approach to the body has led us to devalue the physicality of our being. And it is exactly this kind of thinking that prevents us from being at home in our bodies and imprisons us. We confess as Christians that God's creation is "very good" and that God "becoming body" is at the heart of the gospel, yet we struggle to recognize our embodiment in our own *God-given home*. Let me ask you, when was the last time you properly checked in with your body and consciously engaged with the world around you, using your senses? How often do you give and receive meaningful touch? Touch that connects you with yourself and with others? When did you last smell the scent of a flower or noticed that you, too, have a scent? When did you notice your breathing? Watched a bee doing her work? Let water run through your fingers, wondering how it sustains life, yours included? You get the idea. If we want truly to connect, we need to pay attention to our bodies and make use of our senses: touch, smell, sight, taste, hearing. These are the gateways into fully "living" our life—not thinking. And here we come back to *pleasure*.

The Latin word for savour, *sapor*, means "to taste", and is also the root of *sapientia*, the word for "wisdom".[73] Allowing ourselves to savour and taste is part of how we live and express our sexuality. It is there that we find wisdom that we desperately need. But we can only "taste", "savour" and experience pleasure when we slow down. Think about it. Hastily eating our takeaway meal in front of the TV does not lend itself to notice what it actually tastes like. Sitting on the train whilst playing with a phone allows us completely to ignore the person sitting next to us. You will find your own examples. Ultimately, we cannot meet our deepest desire for Love or experience ourselves to be blessed and connected when we are in a (constant) rush. Peter Scazzero, in his book *The Emotionally Healthy Leader*, dedicates a whole chapter to "slowing down for loving union". Loving union requires deceleration. One way that he identifies as vital in taking the speed out of our lives is a regular Sabbath practice: "Stop work. Enjoy rest. Practice delight. Contemplate God".[74] For twenty-four hours every week. I found Scazzero's definition of Sabbath extremely helpful. When I finally realized that *this* is what Sabbath is about, I was stunned at the generosity of such a gift. For a seventh of my time God *commands* me to stop, rest, delight and connect. I would not have given myself that amount of time! Would you? Are you? Stopping work and enjoying rest means we can listen to our bodies. Without them we cannot practise delight. Do you know in what *your* body delights? What it is that gives you pleasure? Remarkably, Scazzero also draws a connection between shame and Sabbath. He links fear of stopping, or keeping a Sabbath rhythm, with an attitude of shame. We are terrified of what might rise into our consciousness when we completely stop. Our individual "not enough" will rear its head. I can testify how a regular Sabbath practice has positively impacted on my relationship with God and with myself. I am loved by God when I do absolutely nothing for him. I learn to do things which are of no use to anyone.

I play. I savour. I delight in choice food. I rest. I let my body take me wherever she wants to go. Practising Sabbath remains a challenge and requires ongoing readjustments, but I would not want to go without its blessings anymore.

In case you were wondering, we are still talking about sexuality. Tasting, savouring, experiencing pleasure and slowing down for loving union applies to all areas of our lives, sex just being one of them. Expressing ourselves creatively, nurturing our gifts, engaging in caring activities, passing on to others our own learning, all of these activities are part of our being sexual and let us know how we connect with what is "other" in our lives. I learned from Richard Rohr that how we relate to one thing is how we relate to everything.[75] It is just another way of saying that *this* is about *that.*

I love Barbara Brown Taylor's chapter on "The practice of wearing skin" in her book *An Altar in the World.* It is a wonderful approach to honour our bodies as a sacrament. One suggestion of hers that caught my attention is to pray naked in front of a mirror.[76] I imagine this might sound way out of your comfort zone—it did for me, too, when I first came across it. But it just shows how wired we are to thinking *negatively* about our bodies, instead of exploring and connecting with the body we have been given. Why does the suggestion of praying naked make us feel embarrassed? These are our bodies. They are good. They are beautiful. That is what we confess, but not quite what we live. I know!

But try it out and see what happens. You might want to think about dancing and moving, too, praying with the body instead of words. Or treating yourself to a full, therapeutic body massage. Getting your hands dirty in the garden. Go bird watching. Sit by the river. Savour each bite of a well-cooked meal. Such wisdom is available right here and right now. How could we have ever thought that we can live as whole, sexual beings without learning deliberately to "wear our skin", be a bodily being, and "return to our home"?

And now let's apply these explorations to the question of self-pleasure. What if we approached this subject from a similar angle? If we really looked at what actually happens when we masturbate? Are we using it purely in response to our sexual, bodily urges, releasing or trying to get rid of them by self-stimulation until we reach an orgasm? Are we actually trying to escape our bodies when we do this? Are we doing the same when we watch pornography? Why are we engaging with it? Could we instead intentionally explore and become present to our *own* bodies? Could we learn to simply savour when we touch ourselves, without "getting somewhere"? Or mindfully engage with the image of the naked body of another and find out what it is we are looking for? What if we noticed, maybe for the first time, how touching one part of our bodies causes a sensation somewhere else? And how does that sensation travel? Intentionally engaging with our own bodies can be a way of fostering intimacy with ourselves, and therefore with God, and it can, but does not have to include our genitals. Focusing on sensation, the unfolding of a way, rather than on an outcome can be a liberating way of honouring, discovering and owning our bodily self. Trying to achieve peak orgasm so easily becomes like racing on a well-known path to the destination the world has told us we need to reach. (This applies to couples just as much.) Learning to slow down, feeling the pace of touch, staying present to our bodies and our breathing, and noticing what happens, is like finding all the little byways in our body that we have never walked on. Peak orgasms normally release dopamine into our bodies, which gives us a wonderful kick, just as other activities like eating or intense exercise can do. But, similarly to other addictive substances, it causes a "hangover" afterwards. Dopamine is the principal neurochemical that activates our reward system, a driving factor in addictions, and over time it needs more and stronger stimuli to produce the same high. A deliberate, slow and mindful connecting with our body and our breathing in contrast enables a higher release of oxytocin, a "love hormone", promoting trust, empathy and connection.[77] We do not have to go anywhere. We just enjoy the journey. And we do so in the presence of God. Like praying naked in front of a mirror, inviting God into loving and gentle self-touch can be a way of reclaiming our bodies and re-establishing the connection we have lost. You can apply the same approach to a mindful engagement with wholesome food, exercise and other activities. Whenever we open up towards ourselves, to what is really going on, we ultimately become more open towards God and we will increasingly notice what pulls us away from God and ourselves.

Could it be that God *wants* to be invited in our sexual self-pleasure, where we engage with ourselves in a loving way? What is wrong about touching ourselves? What if *you* touched yourself without the aim of getting an orgasm? These kinds of questions might be the first step to questioning our previous way of thinking. We talked about shame resilience. It seems to me that accepting our sexual needs and a conscious practice of loving, mindful self-touch could help in releasing our sense of shame. As so often in life, it is not a matter of what we do, but how and why. *How* do we touch ourselves and *with what intention?* Slowing down, sensing, savouring, practising delight with our own bodies. We need to look.

If masturbation or other ways of self-pleasure become addictive and serve to avoid feeling our loneliness, then we need to find new ways of intimacy and connection. If sexual fantasies take centre stage in our lives, and stop us from praying, then we need to listen and ask why, and what these fantasies are telling us. If there is a risk that our sexual urges will lead to behaviour that questions our commitment or puts others at risk, then we have to act against or leave certain situations—and seek help. Can you see how different this is to "don't go there, it's too dangerous"?

It seems to me that, when it comes to our sexuality, we are invited to take a very personal and unique journey. What helps one to claim more freedom in their expression of sexuality might hinder the other. What is a struggle for you might not be an issue for me. Our individual road towards intimacy and vulnerability, in the embrace of our need for a physical, emotional, spiritual connection and the expression of ourselves, is narrow. We can fall off either side. If pornography, addiction and the potential for abuse are on one side, frigidity, coldness and a life without passion are on the other. And what connects both these sides is a being cut off from our bodily self. Our temptations, and how we try to do our bit (or avoid) handling them will be unique to each of us. One key practice needed to stay on the road is discernment. This is about testing and sifting which of our behaviours lead to an increase in faith, hope and love. Anything that disconnects us, pushes us to withdraw into ourselves, and puts us at the centre of our attention and actions is therefore something that we need to watch and gently correct. We are looking at the fruits in our lives, not "moral perfection". At least this is what I believe Jesus taught. Have a look at Matthew 7:16 and 18:

> By their fruit you will recognise them. Do people pick grapes from thorn-bushes, or figs from thistles? Likewise, every good tree bears good fruit, but a bad tree bears bad fruit. A good

tree cannot bear bad fruit, and a bad tree cannot
bear good fruit.

Reaching out to God in prayer, and also to trusted
companions, in honesty and humility will help us to
grow in taking all our discoveries about our bodies,
needs, desires and sexuality into our relationship with
God. There, we can honestly grieve those things we
have lost. There, we will find forgiveness for our failings,
release from our shame, encouragement for our fears,
and, above all, connection. Remember: we are made
for connection. God will never cut us off, no matter
where we have travelled. Love awaits us always, and to
Love we need to return, without neglecting truth, and
by that, I mean integrity. And it is this Love to which
we ultimately commit as consecrated celibates with our
whole being.

6

Making a commitment

Keeping discernment at the heart of the formation process, we will see whether someone continues to experience a sense of being called to make a commitment to celibacy and grows in freedom and joy. Someone who feels that they are not meant to live out their vocation in the context of a traditional religious order might very likely and eventually ask how such a step can be "formalized" and "made public". For men and women who are rooted in the Anglican tradition and want to submit in their calling to the authority of the Church, this can happen under the cover of the "Single Consecrated Life". A bishop undertakes the ceremony, both for the first, temporary vow that normally spans a period of between one and three years, and then, after further discernment and formation, a life vow.[78] In the Roman Catholic Church, women have the option to seek the rite of consecration under the umbrella of the "Order of the Consecrated Virgins". Those vows are formally recognized under Canon Law, and are accepted by a "legitimate superior", normally a bishop. For a Catholic man who wants to commit to celibacy without entering a religious order, it appears that, in the eyes of the Catholic Church and under canon law, he can only make a private vow, unless he wants to embrace the life of a hermit and make vows accordingly.

And then there are those of us who have never grown up in either the Anglican or Catholic (or Lutheran or Episcopal) Church and have been members of independent churches with a different understanding about what church is and how it is organized, about the role of pastor or priest, ministry, authority, liturgy and rites. If this is you, you might wonder how you can express and make a commitment to consecrated celibacy that honours the gravity and sincerity of your choice.

I would like to offer some thoughts for someone who, after discernment, feels called to take this step, and is pondering these questions.

First, a public vow or commitment can be very affirming and helpful. There is a huge difference between making a promise to yourself in your heart, or even in the presence of one other person, compared with making a vow in public. Bearing in mind how we defined consecrated celibacy, the vow we make needs to express the making of such a commitment as a serious and significant step that involves our whole life. It is made with the intention of it remaining valid for the rest of our lives, even if our first vow is temporary. Making a public vow recognizes the significance of taking this step, and it brings with it an element of accountability. If we do not tell anyone about our commitment, then we can easily walk away from it when life turns out differently from how we anticipated and at the first sight of temptations. A handful of people who know us well and who, in all likelihood, will continue to journey with us, need to know about this commitment. It would be even better if we gave them permission to challenge us when they feel we have become unfaithful to our commitment to Christ. If you consider an analogy with marriage, you will be likely to agree that for such a commitment, it is appropriate and necessary to make the decision public. This is not done in secret or between the two partners alone. An agreement in private is simply not a "marriage".[79] Of course, when we vow to give ourselves to God as consecrated celibates, outside traditional Church or religious orders, this step does not have any *legal* implications (in contrast to marriage). But both spiritually and psychologically, it means nothing less than having accepted and entered into a new state of life. We literally become someone else after making a public vow to remain single and give our whole being to God. We become someone we were not before. This may sound too strong for some, but I can speak for myself and many consecrated celibates I know personally, that making such a commitment causes a shift in our walk with Christ which is hard to put into words. It is here that often only the nuptial metaphor can do it justice: A married couple, whilst being open to others and (hopefully) living in friendships outside their partnership, have formed a union and unit that needs protection, space and time. This necessarily requires some exclusivity, so that the intimacy and trust in the relationship can be deepened. The same is true when a commitment to celibacy is made that has its roots in God's invitation to a union marked by mutuality, as we explored earlier.

It is because of this gravity, that, secondly, I would highly recommend making this promise in a formal way in the presence of others, ideally in the company of mature Christians who understand its significance. Making a promise to God which entails all of our being cannot be left to the "flow of the moment" or how we might feel in terms of choosing the words to mark the occasion, be this promise for one to three years (initially), and later for as long as we live. Equally, the liturgy for consecration should be well prepared and take a significant amount of time. We do not give ourselves to God in that way in five minutes! The language we use needs to be carefully chosen and should be, as much as possible, an accurate expression of *what* we are doing and *why* we are doing it. For me, it took many conversations with my spiritual director on how I would word my promise to God prior to my profession, and this helped me to deepen my understanding.

I wrote a liturgy for a commitment to celibacy for the Northumbria Community's *Celtic Daily Prayer II*, and I have provided this as an appendix at the end of the book. It can be used by anyone who wishes to make a commitment to consecrated celibacy, as I described it earlier.

Making a vow of consecrated celibacy initially for a restricted time is a tried and tested approach, and I would recommend this, even if at the time of my own commitment I struggled with the idea. A temporary vow is always made with the intention of making a life-long vow, but it is good to give ourselves time to explore in some depth whether we can sustain the call and allow it to be tested—and tested it will be! In my experience, such testing often happens quite promptly after a vow is made publicly for the first time. This testing can come in different guises, for we all have areas where we are most easily attacked. But do not be surprised if after making a vow to consecrated celibacy, someone might enter your life you feel attracted to (and/or vice versa). And then the "real" working out of your vocation begins.

Dietrich Bonhoeffer, the German theologian whom I quoted earlier, said that it is marriage that sustains the love of the couple, rather than their love sustaining the marriage. I have found this to be as true of a vow to consecrated celibacy. It is the vow that carries and holds me once it is made. I can return to it time and again, knowing that the promise made is securely held by God, and I can assure you that I had to return to my vow as my anchor in stormy times in my life. Reminding myself that "leaving is not an option" has sustained me when I wondered if I should continue on this chosen path.

As with any commitment, ongoing renewal is required. For the consecrated celibate, this needs to flow out of and consist in a life of prayer, connection with others, and holding our lifestyle and choices before our God. As it is the union with Christ which is at the heart of consecrated celibacy, this union will not lead to navel-gazing or private holiness. The gospel call is always to follow Christ, to take up our cross and to love our neighbour.

The committed, consecrated celibate can reflect God's faithful love in a unique way. Ultimately our deepest longings can only be met in the Love of God, not in a human being, whatever our state in life. Paradoxically, at the same time it embraces the truth that, as long as we live here on this earth, we will *always* live with unmet longing.

We need to keep the wound of our longing *deliberately* open. It is in the experience of our longing that we realize that we were made for more than that which our eyes can see and our hands can hold. True life is always a gift which we receive in part, in fleeting moments of grace, when we experience ourselves as deeply and utterly known, seen and loved in our uniqueness and simultaneously being one with the Other. Such a knowing and loving can happen in the physical uniting of our bodies with that of another, the act of sexual union. Where this happens in a spirit of a true giving of self in vulnerability, connection and intimacy, it is perhaps one of the ways in which we come closest to experiencing union with the Divine. As we have seen, for this to be the case a lot of work is involved for both parties who participate in this mystery. There are no givens. Equally, a conscious opening of oneself as a single person can become the doorway to experiencing the God who knows us, touches us and is with us as no human being ever can. The committed celibate desires to foster this attitude of openness towards the Divine intentionally and regularly, and with the totality of their being. The love affair of a soul with her Maker is a journey of immense beauty and intimacy of which the mystics of all ages bear witness. The ways in which God can touch the core of our being where S/He mysteriously abides, transcends words. This is available to all of us, no matter the state in life in which we find ourselves. But, as I said, just as a formal commitment to a partner and a public vow in marriage brings about a shift in the relationship between the two who enter into it, committing to a covenantal relationship with God will inevitably cause shifts and changes, both in the person making that vow and in the spiritual realm. We therefore must not underestimate the power of making a public promise.

This does not mean that from then on "they lived happily ever after". We all come with our unique brokenness and carry this into all our relationships, both with the human and the Divine. We rely heavily on God's grace, no matter who we are and what we are called to be. Sometimes the acknowledgement of our brokenness can mean realizing that what, once upon a time, we perceived as God's calling and gift, ultimately might no longer be for us. None of us know how our lives will turn out and what will occur on our journey. We can only follow what we perceive as God's invitation at the time and give it our best shot, give our *all* to explore and live out what that means for us.

Conclusion

I trust that this book has made it abundantly clear that life as a committed celibate is not a "holier" way of living in comparison to marriage or being single. Yet neither is marriage the "default" state in life which God has in mind for us. Traditionally, consecrated celibacy has been *the* touchstone of religious (monastic) life, and the most ancient of its meanings was simply the complete giving of oneself to the person of Christ, irrespective of joining a particular community or participating in specific ministries. In these current times, where people increasingly struggle with institutionalized religion and a new monastic movement is gathering momentum, this provides us with a great opportunity to discover anew what lies at the heart of a commitment to celibacy.

As we have seen, throughout the centuries people have responded to such a call, in movements of all kinds and shapes, lay or religious, highly organized or with less structure, in stable communities or as hermits living in one place, or wandering the road, for the sake of Christ. The calling is a *charism*, alongside other God-given gifts for the sake of the Body of Christ. Any gift that God gives is for the good of others. It has an outward looking focus and includes an element of serving the wider world. Some find and live this particular giftedness quietly within their inner being, without anyone even telling them what it is they are carrying. But others may never find it until it is given a voice and the voice is heard. What a loss it would be, for them and the Body of Christ, not to do so. We must not underestimate how important it is to name and give language to our experiences of the Divine. It is only then that we can begin to make sense of the call and welcome it. Yes, of course, God is Sovereign, but have we not all experienced that some experiences remain inaccessible to us until someone else speaks of it? This was exactly what Archbishop Justin Welby said about the new monastic life: "If you have not heard about it, it does not exist."[80]

That is why I want to ask: where is the recognition and celebration of the charism of "consecrated celibacy"—in our churches and communities, particularly in the new monastic movement? We aspire to follow the examples of the "wise and the good", as we sing in Evening Prayer of the Northumbria Community. But let us not ignore the fact that so many of "the wise and the good" were living as consecrated celibates. Let us *intentionally* acknowledge their state in life, name it and encourage people to explore it as a real option for their lives. There is no need to emphasize it, let alone make it central in the new monastic movement or in our churches. But just as God seems to stir people to seek out the "pathways of old" with regards to the monastic life, and how this is being rediscovered and reimagined in this day and age, so also I believe that God wants to highlight that for some people this journey includes a commitment to celibacy. Therefore, simply making people aware that consecrated celibacy is something God is still calling people to *today*, and within our midst, would constitute a significant shift in our approach and communication.

As I have mentioned, I have come across an increasing number of people who feel drawn to make such a commitment but know that living in a traditional religious community is not for them. Having met someone who took this step before me, this choice was made more available to me. That is why I hope that those who want to explore such a path will discover this book and find it a source of encouragement. If this is you, I hope it will show you that you are not alone on this journey. The appendix contains material that aims to support you in your explorations.

This resource might also enable the new monastic movement to identify more easily those among their people who carry this gift within them but have not been able to name and openly embrace it for their lives. And, lastly, having taken a "fresh look at an ancient vocation", I hope that this can assist churches and spiritual directors in accompanying those who feel drawn to explore consecrated celibacy for themselves.

Earlier in this book, I shared Gerald May's definition of "consecration". I would like to close with another quote of his. May has a way of pinpointing truths that make my heart sing. When I read this, there is a recognition of our continued journeying within ourselves and God's endless invitations towards freedom and expansion. What love, what homecoming, for all of us! Throughout the centuries, people have tried to find their way of responding, and some have done so in making the commitment to consecrated celibacy. Very interestingly, May has placed these explorations in his book *Addiction and Grace*. I think that puts them right where they belong: in the midst of the messiness and ongoing struggles in our lives to follow the God we love, and to be transformed by this love:

> Consecration means dedication to God. It occurs when we claim our deepest desire for God, beneath, above, and beyond all other things. (...) In consecration we dedicate our struggle to something more; consecration is our assent to God's transforming grace, our commitment homeward. In the beginning, we will not understand the full meaning of consecration. Perhaps, in this life, we never will. Nor will we comprehend the ups and downs, the joys and agonies of the journey that must follow. And certainly we will be unable to grasp the overarching cosmic meaning of our small assent, the joy it gives to God, the deepening love it will bring to humanity, the universal

covenant it has enriched. We may not have any idea that consecration means encounter with spaciousness, that an unconditioned reality awaits our conditioned mind. But our yes comes from some taste, some bare recollection of all these things. We know it has something to do with home. There is love in it and hope. We feel a small breeze of freedom. And in the tiny space our hearts can say yes.[81]

Questions for discernment

- Have I been called to consecrated celibacy?
- How has the idea to make such a commitment come about?
- *How* did I hear this call to give my whole being to Christ in this particular way?
- When? Did it come as a surprise or has a confidence about this vocation quietly grown over the years?
- Is it a combination of both? Can I trace back the beginnings of a sense of being called?
- What was my reaction to feeling invited to make such a choice?
- Have I met consecrated celibates, and what are my thoughts and fantasies about this state of life?
- Have I ever pondered entering a religious order?
- What is and has been my relationship to the Divine, and, in particular, to the person of Christ?
- Can I sense that I have a choice? Do I feel that saying "yes" or "no" would diminish God's love for me?
- How would I describe my own psychological, spiritual, emotional, physical and social wellbeing

in life? How does my own upbringing and wounding experienced in my family of origin and significant relationships influence my wish to commit to consecrated celibacy, as far as I can tell now?

- Do I have issues with addiction? Do I suffer from chronic health problems, and how do they impact my daily life and my relationship with God?

- How do I manage in daily life? Am I engaged in regular, paid work? If not, what is the background for that?

- Do I have close friendships in which I can experience intimacy and closeness? Who are my friends? For how long have I known them? Is there a pattern in my way of relating to others?

Vocational discernment questions around our sexuality

- How have I experienced sex and sexuality in my life, beginning with my family of origin?
- Was there ever open talk about it?
- Did my parents or parental figures display affection and tenderness, with each other, with me and my siblings?
- Or was there a shame filled silence around anything to do with sex?
- Was there abuse and violence?

- What was the attitude towards the body, *my* body?
- How did I experience my own gender and what were the messages I heard?
- What was I told is "masculine" and what is "feminine"?
- Did I ever see a naked body? Was I free to be naked?
- How did I experience touch?
- What did I wear?
- Did we speak about feelings in our family and how were my feelings validated?
- How was I helped to navigate puberty, the changes in my body, the awakening of desires for genital sexuality?
- What happened in my first sexual encounters? What relationships did I have with those with whom I became sexually involved?
- Did I avoid any sexual relationship? Why?
- You can take these questions and apply them to your experiences at school, your peer relations, relationship with authority, at university, at work … They will help you open up this terrain and see where you are currently at.
- How do I feel in my body now?
- What role do my sexual experiences play in my wanting to stay single?
- Am I confident about my sexual orientation?
- Am I comfortable with my gender?

- What is my attitude towards masturbation? What happens when I masturbate?
- What happens in my sexual fantasies? What do they tell me about myself, my needs and desires?
- Do I engage with pornography? What happens when I do? What is the need behind it?
- What do I *like* about sex?
- How do I practise pleasure in my life?
- What is my attitude towards eating? What is my relationship with food?
- How do I feel about my need for touch? Where do I receive meaningful touch?
- How do I connect with creation?
- What happens when I stop and rest?
- How do I express my creativity? Which creative activities do I engage with?
- What about my desire to have children?
- How do I express my need for generativity?
- How do I express nurture and care—in relation to myself, my friends, family, creation . . . ?

Liturgy for a commitment to consecrated celibacy

This liturgy also has been published as part of the Northumbria Community's *Celtic Daily Prayer II*.

It is for:

- those who want to give themselves to God in celibacy for a particular period of time;
- those who after testing and discerning with others have come to the conclusion that this is for as long as they shall live.

The Welcome (said by a minister/spiritual director/ mentor)

[Name ...], we are here to celebrate and pray God's blessing upon you in your commitment to celibacy. As friends and sojourners who have walked with you, we pray for ourselves that we let ourselves be loved and

whole-heartedly offer our lives to God, the source of all Love. As the Apostle John says in his first letter: "We love, for God first loved us".

We will keep before us the deepening and strengthening of your commitment, encouraging you to hold on to the God who works in you and us to will and to act according to God's good purpose.

The Affirmation (said by the Group which gathers)

We believe in one God, who is a mystery of relationship, a union of love between Father, Son, and Holy Spirit.

Created by God, we are bearers of the divine image. Whether married or single, our bodies tell us that the story of redemption is one of union: At the core of our being, we all long for union with God, our Creator, Redeemer and Sustainer; and so we pray: You have made us for yourself, O Lord, and our hearts are restless until they rest in you.

We rejoice with you, [*name*], and celebrate the gift of celibacy that God has given you. May your commitment be a sign and witness to us that in God's eternal kingdom we all one day will be one with God and each other in a way that is beyond our understanding.

Time of bearing witness to the journey of wanting to make a commitment to celibacy by the initiate and somebody who has journeyed with them such as their spiritual director, minister, pastor, friend or mentor.

The Declaration

Here, the initiate can express his/her own prayer.

Reading of Scripture (optional verses below)

The Blessing (said by minister/spiritual director/mentor)

Dear *[name]*

Today, you are giving yourself to your beloved God in your commitment to celibacy. As you do this, may you realize that God has known and loved you in a way surpassing anything that you can imagine. You have been loved before anyone even had thought of you or spoken your name.

You are giving yourself up to God in faith. Let your life be built on this faith as on an invisible foundation and let it carry you like a child in its mother's womb.

Your commitment to stay celibate for the sake of God's Kingdom will draw you into the loneliness of the cross of Christ and reveal the basic loneliness that all humans share. Through your being you are called to be a witness to the truth that our deepest longings can only be met in the love of God. At the same time your choice invites you to seek and grow in community, which is built on God's faithfulness. Be careful not to be isolated. Be open to the joys of intimate relationships and foster a mature development of your emotions and human warmth in your life.

In your commitment, you are bringing your potential for love into the new and unlimited fruitfulness of the Kingdom. As you allow your desire for union to lead you deeply into God's heart and solidarity with humankind, you will grow and bear fruit both in your prayer and serving. In that way you will become a mother and father for many.

Let silence guard and seal your heart, God's dwelling place within you.

[*name*], we bless you as you commit yourself to celibacy* in order to give yourself undivided to the love of Christ and to be available in God's kingdom.

*(the following could be added: for a period of ... years/ so long as you shall live)

May you know and live in God's love as you continue your journey with Jesus Christ, who dwells in your heart through the Holy Spirit. Amen.

Possible Scripture readings

I will betroth you to me forever;
I will betroth you in righteousness and
    justice, in love and compassion.
I will betroth you in faithfulness,
And you will acknowledge the Lord.

Hosea 2:19–20

My lover has gone down to his garden,
    to the beds of spices,
to browse in the gardens
    and to gather lilies.
I am my lover's and my lover is mine;
    he browses among the lilies.

Song of Songs 6:2–3

I belong to my beloved,
    and his desire is for me.

Song of Songs 7:10

The Lord your God is with you,
    the Mighty Warrior who saves.
He will take great delight in you;
    in his love he will no longer rebuke you,
    but will rejoice over you with singing.

Zephaniah 3:17

Bibliography

Adams, Ian, *Cave Refectory Road: Monastic Rhythms for Contemporary Living* (Norwich: Canterbury Press, 2010).

Aune, Kristin, *Single Women: Challenge to the Church?* (Carlisle: Paternoster Press, 2002).

Bell, Rob, *Sex God: Exploring the Endless Connections between Sexuality and Spirituality* (Grand Rapids, MI: Zondervan, 2007).

Bonhoeffer, Dietrich, *Nachfolge* (Munich: Kaiser, 1981). ET: *The Cost of Discipleship*, tr. H. Fuller (London: SCM Press, 1959).

Bourgeault, Cynthia, *The Wisdom Jesus: Transforming Heart and Mind: A New Perspective on Christ and his Message* (Boston, MA: Shambhala, 2008).

Brown, Brene, *Daring Greatly: How the Courage to be Vulnerable Transforms the Way We Live, Love, Parent and Lead* (London: Portfolio Penguin, 2013).

Brown Taylor, Barbara, *An Altar in the World: Finding the Sacred Beneath Our Feet* (Norwich: Canterbury Press, 2009).

Clark, Keith, *Being Sexual . . . and Celibate*
(Notre Dame, IN: Ave Maria Press, 1986).

Coakley, Sarah, *The New Asceticism:*
Sexuality, Gender and the Quest for God
(London: Bloomsbury, 2015).

Couvela, Stephanie, *Celebrating Celibacy:*
Sexuality, Intimacy and Wholeness for the Single
Adult (Cambridge: Grove Books, 2007).

Danylak, Barry, *Redeeming Singleness: How*
the Storyline of Scripture Affirms the Single
Life (Wheaton, IL: Crossway, 2010).

Dominian, Jack, *Let's Make Love: The*
Meaning of Sexual Intercourse (London:
Darton, Longman and Todd, 2001).

Eichler, Astrid, *Es muss was anderes*
geben: Lebensperspektiven für Singles
(Wuppertal: Brockhaus Verlag, 2006).

Eldrige, John, *The Journey of Desire* (Nashville,
TN: Thomas Nelson, 2000).

Fox, Matthew, *Original Blessing*
(Santa Fe: Bear, 1990).

Hein, Tim, *Understanding Sexual Abuse*
(Edinburgh: Muddy Pearl, 2018).

Hereford, Amy, CSJ *Religious Life at the*
Crossroads: A School for Mystics and
Prophets (Maryknoll, NY: Orbis, 2013).

Kelly, Geffrey B. and Nelson, F. Burton (eds),
A Testament to Freedom: The Essential
Writings of Dietrich Bonhoeffer (San
Francisco: HarperCollins, 1990).

May, Gerald G., *Addiction and Grace: Love and Spirituality in the Healing of Addictions* (New York: HarperCollins, 1988).

May, Gerald G., *The Awakened Heart: Opening Yourself to the Love You Need* (New York: HarperCollins, 1993).

Monk Kidd, Sue, *The Book of Longings* (London: Tinder Press, 2020).

Müller, Wunnibald, *Liebe und Zölibat: Wie eheloses Leben gelingen kann* (Ostfildern: Grünewald, 2012).

Müller, Wunnibald, *Vom Kusse seines Mundes trunken: Sexualität als Quelle der Spiritualität* (Ostfildern: Grünewald, 2012).

Nouwen, Henri J. M., *Reaching Out: The Three Movements of the Spiritual Life* (London: Fount, 1998).

O'Donohue, John, *Anam Cara: A Book of Celtic Wisdom* (New York: Cliff Street Books, 1997).

Rohr, Richard, *Eager to Love: The Alternative Way of Francis of Assisi* (London: Hodder & Stoughton, 2014).

Ruffing, Janet, R.S.M. *Spiritual Direction: Beyond the Beginnings* (Mahwah, NJ: Paulist Press, 2000).

Scazzero, Peter, *The Emotionally Healthy Leader: How Transforming Your Inner Life Will Deeply Transform Your Church, Team, and the World* (Grand Rapids, MI: Zondervan, 2015).

Schneiders, Sandra M., I.H.M. *Selling All: Commitment, Consecrated Celibacy and Community in Catholic Religious Life* [vol. ii of *Religious Life in a New Millennium*] (Mahwah, NJ: Paulist Press, 2001).

Schütz, Paul, *Warum ich noch ein Christ bin: Briefe an einen jungen Freund* (Berlin: Hans von Hugo und Schlotheim, 1937; Munich: Pattloch, 1996).

Sellner, Edward C., *Introduction to Wisdom of the Celtic Saints* (Felton: Northumbria Community, 1993).

Sheldrake, Philip, *Spirituality: A Brief History* (2nd edn, Chichester: Wiley-Blackwell, 2013).

Simpson, Ray, *High Street Monasteries: Fresh Expressions of Committed Christianity* (Bury St Edmunds: Kevin Mayhew Ltd., 2009).

Stewart, Columba, OSB "Rethinking the History of Monasticism East and West: A Modest *tour d'horizon*", in Bhattacharji, Santha, Williams, Rowan and Mattos, Dominic (eds), *Prayer and Thought in Monastic Tradition: Essays in Honour of Benedicta Ward SLG* (London: Bloomsbury, 2014), pp. 3–16.

Swan, Laura, *The Wisdom of the Beguines: The Forgotten Story of a Medieval Women's Movement* (Katonah, NY: BlueBridge, 2016).

Valters Paintner, Christine, *The Wisdom of the Body: A Contemplative Journey to Wholeness for Women* (Notre Dame, IN: Sorin Books, 2017).

Wharton, Kate, *Single-Minded: Being Single, Whole and Living Life to the Full* (Oxford: Monarch Books, 2013).

Wilson-Hartgrove, Jonathan, *New Monasticism: What It Has to Say to Today's Church* (Grand Rapids, MI: Brazos, 2008).

Notes

1 There is, of course, a rather large amount of literature available on new monasticism. Some of the titles are: Ian Adams, *Cave Refectory Road: Monastic Rhythms for Contemporary Living* (Norwich: Canterbury Press, 2010); Jonathan Wilson-Hartgrove, *New Monasticism: What It Has to Say to Today's Church* (Grand Rapids, MI: Brazos, 2008); Ray Simpson, *High Street Monasteries: Fresh Expressions of Committed Christianity* (Bury St Edmunds: Kevin Mayhew Ltd., 2009).

2 Geffrey B. Kelly and F. Burton Nelson (eds), *A Testament to Freedom: The Essential Writings of Dietrich Bonhoeffer* (San Francisco: HarperCollins, 1990), p. 424. Bonhoeffer makes this comment in a letter written to his brother Karl-Friedrich Bonhoeffer from London on 14 January 1935.

3 Dietrich Bonhoeffer, *Nachfolge* (Munich: Chr. Kaiser Verlag, 1981), p. 17. My translation, as I have found that the translation as it is used in Dietrich Bonhoeffer, *The Cost of Discipleship* (London: SCM Press, 1959), p. 6 is inaccurate in a crucial place and therefore gives the whole paragraph a meaning which was not intended by Bonhoeffer.

4 Bonhoeffer, *Nachfolge*, pp. 18–27.

5 See for example Kristin Aune, *Single Women: Challenge to the Church?* (Carlisle: Paternoster Press, 2002). In her study, Aune discovered common struggles and themes of single women in a church context.

It makes interesting reading and provides evidence that my statement about the "comments by well-meaning people" is not purely based on anecdotal knowledge and my own experience. Kate Wharton, herself an Anglican priest, goes as far as to say that the church is "marriage-obsessed": *Single-Minded: Being Single, Whole and Living Life to the Full* (Oxford: Monarch Books, 2013), p. 49.

6   I have read, with great interest, Sue Monk Kidd's latest novel, *The Book of Longings* (London: Tinder Press, 2020), which tells the story of the imaginary wife of Jesus. If we allow ourselves to imagine this as a possibility, in my view, it does not take away anything of what I am writing about in this book. As we will see later, the biblical narrative clearly includes and affirms the possibility of a happy and full life as a single person.

7   Richard Rohr, "Aliveness", *Trinity: Part One, Daily Meditations* (10 May 2019), Centre for Action and Contemplation <https://cac.org/aliveness-2019-05-10/>, accessed 6 December 2021.

8   Although Bowlby's attachment theory has been refined since its first inception, its basic finding that the forming of attachments to our primary caregivers are vital for our future development is still relevant today.

9   Barry Danylak, *Redeeming Singleness: How the Storyline of Scripture Affirms the Single Life* (Wheaton, IL: Crossway, 2010), pp. 80–1.

10   Danylak, *Redeeming Singleness*, pp. 138–9.

11   See Danylak, *Redeeming Singleness*, pp. 179–83.

12   In his explorations on "Discipleship and the Individual", Bonhoeffer speaks about Christ calling men and women out of the "immediacies of the world", Christ being the Mediator "who has come between us and the world", and therefore, "his followers have no more immediate realities of their own", including their family relationships (Bonhoeffer,

Nachfolge, pp. 70–1). Whilst not agreeing with all of Bonhoeffer's conclusions, I can see the point he is trying to make that the claim that family life can put on us, particularly when our relations do not share our faith, can quite easily come between us and Christ's call.

[13] Astrid Eichler, *Es muss was anderes geben: Lebensperspektiven für Singles* (Wuppertal: Brockhaus Verlag, 2006), p. 34, my translation.

[14] John Eldrige, *The Journey of Desire* (Nashville, TN: Thomas Nelson, 2000), p. 141.

[15] Danylak, *Redeeming Singleness*, p. 152.

[16] Columba Stewart, OSB, "Rethinking the History of Monasticism East and West: A Modest *tour d'horizon*", in Santha Bhattacharji, Rowan Williams, and Dominic Mattos (eds), *Prayer and Thought in Monastic Tradition: Essays in Honour of Benedicta Ward SLG* (London: Bloomsbury, 2014), pp. 3–16, here at pp. 4–10.

[17] Philip Sheldrake, *Spirituality: A Brief History* (2nd edn, Chichester: Wiley-Blackwell, 2013), p. 16.

[18] Gerald G. May points out that the Desert Fathers and Mothers believed in authentic asceticism which was quite ordinary and not associated with extremes of self-mortification. See Gerald May, *Addiction and Grace: Love and Spirituality in the Healing of Addictions* (New York: HarperCollins, 1988), p. 141. Thomas Merton says the same when he states: "The Desert Fathers later acquired a reputation for fanaticism because of the stories that were told about their ascetic feats by indiscreet admirers. They were indeed ascetics: but when we read their own words and see what they themselves thought about life, we find that they were anything but fanatics", *The Wisdom of the Desert* (New York: New Directions, 1970), p. 14. In contrast, Jack Dominian believes that control over the body was the preoccupation of the desert monks: "The desert ascetic did not flourish with just control over his

mind. His body also had to be tutored and in bringing the body under control the soul was influenced", *Let's Make Love: The Meaning of Sexual Intercourse* (London: Darton, Longman and Todd, 2001), p. 18.

[19] Sheldrake, *Spirituality*, p. 53 and p. 56.

[20] Sheldrake, *Spirituality*, p. 51 in reference to Acts 6:1–6 and 1 Timothy 5:3–16.

[21] Sandra M. Schneiders, I.H.M., *Selling All: Commitment, Consecrated Celibacy and Community in Catholic Religious Life* [vol. ii of *Religious Life in a New Millennium*] (Mahwah, NJ: Paulist Press, 2001), p. 166.

[22] Schneiders, *Selling All*, p. 166. Schneiders' explorations of the difference in men's and women's sexuality and subsequent approach to consecrated celibacy are enlightening, and I highly recommend these to anyone who is exploring a call to consecrated celibacy.

[23] Sheldrake, *Spirituality*, p. 56.

[24] Edward C. Sellner, *Introduction to Wisdom of the Celtic Saints* (Felton: Northumbria Community, 1993), p. 11.

[25] Amy Hereford, CSJ, *Religious Life at the Crossroads: A School for Mystics and Prophets* (Maryknoll, NY: Orbis Books, 2013), pp. 8–9.

[26] Laura Swan, *The Wisdom of the Beguines: The Forgotten Story of a Medieval Women's Movement* (Katonah: BlueBridge, 2016), p. 60.

[27] Swan, *The Wisdom of the Beguines*, pp. 58–61.

[28] Sheldrake, *Spirituality*, p. 84.

[29] A website hosted by Paul and Karen Fredette, an American couple who have embraced a life of solitude and silence. "Karen spent thirty years as a Poor Clare nun in Canton, Ohio. Paul was a member of the Glenmary Home Missioners for twenty years", <http://www.ravensbreadministries.com/>, accessed 6 December 2021.

[30] Schneiders, *Selling All*, p. 120.

31   Olivia Rudgard "Consecrated Virgins need not be virgins says Vatican", *Daily Telegraph*, 16 July 2018 <https://www.telegraph.co.uk/news/2018/07/16/consecrated-virgins-need-not-virgins-says-vatican/>, accessed 6 December 2021.

32   "CONSECRATED Virgins", The Website of the National Office for Vocation, <https://www.ukvocation.org/?page_id=113>, accessed 6 December 2021.

33   Single Consecrated Life: A fresh expression of religious life in the Anglican Church <http://www.singleconsecratedlife-anglican.org.uk/>, accessed 6 December 2021.

34   <https://arlyb.org.uk/community/melanesian-brotherhood-mbh/>, accessed 11 March 2022.

35   Stephanie Couvela, *Celebrating Celibacy: Sexuality, Intimacy and Wholeness for the Single Adult* (Cambridge: Grove Books, 2007), p. 6. I appreciate Couvela's explorations and conclusions around intimacy and wholeness for a person who is not consciously engaging in genital sexual activity with another person outside marriage. Much of what she has to say applies to a person who has made a commitment to stay single. I do not believe, however, that choosing the term "celibate" for any single Christian will solve the problematic issues that she identifies in the Church's dealings with single people, and which I looked at earlier.

36   Schneiders, *Selling All*, p. 128.

37   Schneiders, *Selling All*, p. 153.

38   Janet Ruffing, R.S.M., *Spiritual Direction: Beyond the Beginnings* (Mahwah, NJ: Paulist Press, 2000), p. 127.

39   Schneiders, *Selling All*, p. 157, and also p. 29.

40   Hereford, *Religious Life at the Crossroads*, p. 130.

41 Gerald G. May, *The Awakened Heart: Opening Yourself to the Love You Need* (New York: HarperCollins, 1993), p. 65.

42 Schneiders, *Selling All*, p. 14.

43 Schneiders, *Selling All*, p. 14.

44 Schneiders, *Selling All*, p. 15.

45 *Spiritual Direction: Beyond the Beginnings* (Janet Ruffing, R.S.M.), has very valuable explorations in that regard, particularly in Chapter 4, "Love Mysticism in Spiritual Direction" and Chapter 5, "Mutuality with God".

46 This is David Fleming's (SJ) contemporary translation of St Ignatius' 3rd Part of the "First Principle and Foundation" for the Spiritual Exercises: <https://www.ignatianspirituality.com/what-the-principle-and-foundation-calls-us-to/>, accessed 7 December 2021.

47 Schneiders, *Selling All*, p. 56.

48 See for example: Professor Liz Kelly, Kairika Karsna, *Measuring the scale and changing nature of child sexual abuse and child sexual exploitation Scoping report, July 2017 updated August 2018.* Centre of expertise on sexual abuse (CSA Centre): <https://www.csacentre.org.uk/documents/scale-and-nature-scoping-report-2018/>, accessed 7 December 2021. Or Tim Hein, *Understanding Sexual Abuse* (Edinburgh: Muddy Pearl, 2018), p. xiii.

49 Paul Schütz, *Warum ich noch ein Christ bin: Briefe an einen jungen Freund* (Berlin: Hans von Hugo und Schlotheim, 1937; Munich: Pattloch, 1996), p. 79, my translation.

50 The Catholic Church recognizes that some single people are called to a commitment to life-long celibacy and, although there is no official confirmation process for this calling, uses the term "apostolic celibacy" to describe this vocation. It acknowledges that "this is a real vocation

and is of increasing significance in the life of the Church". <http://www.ukvocation.org/?page_id=52>, accessed 7 December 2021.

[51] Sarah Coakley, *The New Asceticism: Sexuality, Gender and the Quest for God* (London: Bloomsbury, 2015), p. 51.

[52] Cynthia Bourgeault, *The Wisdom Jesus* (Boston: Shambhala, 2008), p. 79.

[53] Bourgeault, *The Wisdom Jesus*, p. 78.

[54] Personal email from Richard Rohr, 20 August 2014.

[55] Rob Bell, *Sex God: Exploring the Endless Connections between Sexuality and Spirituality* (Grand Rapids, MI: Zondervan, 2007), p. 15.

[56] Bell, *Sex God*, p. 19.

[57] Wunnibald Müller, *Vom Kusse seines Mundes trunken: Sexualität als Quelle der Spiritualität* (Ostfildern: Grünewald, 2012), p. 19, my translation.

[58] Ruffing, *Spiritual Direction*, p. 133.

[59] Matthew Fox, *Original Blessing*, (Santa Fe: Bear, 1990), p. 52.

[60] Christine Valters Paintner, *The Wisdom of the Body: A Contemplative Journey to Wholeness for Women* (Notre Dame: Sorin Books, 2017), p. 76–7.

[61] Brene Brown, *Daring Greatly: How the Courage to be Vulnerable Transforms the Way We Live, Love, Parent and Lead* (London: Portfolio Penguin, 2013), p. 8.

[62] Keith Clark, Capuchin, *Being Sexual ... and Celibate* (Notre Dame: Ave Maria Press, 1986), p. 41.

[63] Richard Rohr, *Eager to Love: The Alternative Way of Francis of Assisi* (London: Hodder & Stoughton, 2014), p. 8.

[64] Henri J. M. Nouwen, *Reaching Out: The Three Movements of the Spiritual Life* (London: Fount, 1998), p. 13.

[65] Brown, *Daring Greatly*, p. 41.

66   Brown, *Daring Greatly*, p. 69.

67   Clark, *Being Sexual … and Celibate*, p. 76.

68   Clark, *Being Sexual … and Celibate*, p. 128.

69   Ruffing, *Spiritual Direction*, p. 44.

70   Wunnibald Müller, *Liebe und Zölibat: Wie eheloses Leben gelingen kann* (Ostfildern: Matthias Grünewald, 2012), p. 63, my translation.

71   Müller, *Liebe und Zölibat,* p. 65.

72   John O'Donohue, *Anam Cara: A Book of Celtic Wisdom* (New York: Cliff Street Books, 1997), p. 48.

73   Valters Paintner, *The Wisdom of the Body*, p. 56.

74   Peter Scazzero, *The Emotionally Healthy Leader* (Grand Rapids, MI: Zondervan, 2015), p. 144.

75   Richard Rohr, "Reuniting our separated selves", *Gender and Sexuality: Week One, Daily Meditations*, (17 April 2018), Centre for Action and Contemplation <https://cac.org/reuniting-our-separated-selves-2018-04-17/>, accessed 7 December 2021.

76   Barbara Brown Taylor, *An Altar in the World: Finding the Sacred Beneath Our Feet* (Norwich: Canterbury Press, 2009), p. 37.

77   Sexual Health Site: Practical information about human sexuality, relationships and spirituality. *The Dark Side of the Big "O"*, 1 April 2011 <https://www.sexualhealthsite.info/the-dark-side-of-the-big-o.php>, accessed 7 December 2021.

78   See the sections on discernment and profession at <https://www.singleconsecratedlife-anglican.org.uk/>, accessed 8 December 2021.

79   Jack Dominian points out that this understanding of marriage only started after 1564 in the Catholic Church, and in the Anglican Church in England and Wales after 1754, "when a ceremony in church before a priest and two witnesses became essential". Prior to that, the essentials of marriage were (and in his opinion should still be) "free

consent, meaning commitment, and sexual intercourse, meaning consummation". Jack Dominian, *Let's Make Love: The Meaning of Sexual Intercourse* (London: Darton, Longman and Todd, 2001), p. 107.

[80] Archbishop Justin Welby, during a New Monastic Community Conference at Lambeth Palace in October 2018; handwritten notes by the author.

[81] Gerald G. May, *Addiction and Grace: Love and Spirituality in the Healing of Addictions* (New York: HarperCollins, 1993), p. 150.

Lightning Source UK Ltd.
Milton Keynes UK
UKHW022309160223
417143UK00014B/438